THE
HIDDEN HISTORY *of*
NEOLIBERALISM

HOW REAGANISM GUTTED AMERICA AND HOW TO RESTORE ITS GREATNESS

THOM HARTMANN

BK

Berrett–Koehler Publishers, Inc.

The great innovation of Hayek and Mises was to create a defense of the free market using the language of freedom and revolutionary change.... Even as the welfare state and the mixed economy were coming into existence, Hayek and Mises set as their political imperative tearing them down.

—Kim Phillips-Fein, *Invisible Hands: The Businessmen's Crusade Against the New Deal*

Neoliberal democracy, ... [i]nstead of citizens, it produces consumers. Instead of communities, it produces shopping malls. The net result is an atomized society of disengaged individuals who feel demoralized and socially powerless. In sum, neoliberalism is the immediate and foremost enemy of genuine participatory democracy, not just in the United States but across the planet, and will be for the foreseeable future.

—Robert W. McChesney, introduction to *Profit Over People: Neoliberalism and Global Order*, by Noam Chomsky

Berrett-Koehler Publishers, Inc.
1333 Broadway, Suite 1000
Oakland, CA 94612-1921
Tel: (510) 817-2277; Fax: (510) 817-2278
www.bkconnection.com

ORDERING INFORMATION
Quantity sales. Special discounts are available on quantity purchases by corporations, associations, and others. For details, contact the "Special Sales Department" at the Berrett-Koehler address above.
Individual sales. Berrett-Koehler publications are available through most bookstores. They can also be ordered directly from Berrett-Koehler: Tel: (800) 929-2929; Fax: (802) 864-7626; www.bkconnection.com.
Orders for college textbook / course adoption use. Please contact Berrett-Koehler: Tel: (800) 929-2929; Fax: (802) 864-7626.

Distributed to the U.S. trade and internationally by Penguin Random House Publisher Services.

Berrett-Koehler and the BK logo are registered trademarks of Berrett-Koehler Publishers, Inc.

Printed in the United States of America

Berrett-Koehler books are printed on long-lasting acid-free paper. When it is available, we choose paper that has been manufactured by environmentally responsible processes. These may include using trees grown in sustainable forests, incorporating recycled paper, minimizing chlorine in bleaching, or recycling the energy produced at the paper mill.

Library of Congress Cataloging-in-Publication Data
Names: Hartmann, Thom, 1951 – author.
Title: The hidden history of neoliberalism : how reaganism gutted America and how to restore its greatness / Thom Hartmann.
Description: First Edition. | Oakland, CA : Berrett-Koehler Publishers, 2022. | Series: The hidden history series | Includes bibliographical references and index.
Identifiers: LCCN 2022009312 (print) | LCCN 2022009313 (ebook) | ISBN 9781523002320 (paperback) | ISBN 9781523002337 (pdf) | ISBN 9781523002344 (epub) | ISBN 9781523002351
Subjects: LCSH: Neoliberalism—United States—History. | United States—Economic policy. | Free trade—United States—History. | Liberty—United States—History. | Oligarchy—United States—History.
Classification: LCC HB95 .H3647 2022 (print) | LCC HB95 (ebook) | DDC 320.51/3—dc23/eng/20220228
LC record available at https://lccn.loc.gov/2022009312
LC ebook record available at https://lccn.loc.gov/2022009313

First Edition
28 27 26 25 24 23 22   10 9 8 7 6 5 4 3 2 1

Book production: Linda Jupiter Productions   *Cover design:* Wes Youssi, M.80 Design
Edit: Elissa Rabellino   *Interior design:* Good Morning Graphics
Proofread: Mary Kanable   *Index:* Paula C. Durbin-Westby

CONTENTS

FOREWORD by Greg Palast   vii

INTRODUCTION: The Plot to Save the World   1
1.   Save Us from the Utopians   7
2.   The Birth of Neoliberalism   13
3.   Neoliberalism's Fathers: Mises, Hayek, and Friedman   19
     Ludwig von Mises and the "Critical Race Theory"
     of Neoliberalism   19
     F. A. Hayek vs. the Birth of Democratic Socialism   22
     Milton Friedman   30
4.   Neoliberalism Goes to Work   36
5.   Worldwide Neoliberalism Experiments   41
6.   Milton Friedman Hearts General Pinochet   42
7.   Neoliberalism Comes to America   51
8.   Bill Clinton Hearts the Neoliberal Revolution   60
9.   George W. Bush Pushes Neoliberalism Even Further   68
10. Neoliberalism Blows Up in Bush's Face   74
11. Obama Rescues Neoliberalism from Itself   79
12. Trump Attacks Neoliberalism   81
13. Biden Challenges Neoliberalism's Core Concepts   83
14. How Neoliberalism Changed America in 40 Years   84
     Taxes   84
     Trade   85
     Health Care   88
     Education and Higher Education   89
     Finance   90
     Employment   91
     Homelessness   92

	Inflation	93
	Media and News	94
	The Environment	96
15.	Privatizing the Commons	98
16.	Destruction of Democracy	106
17.	Breaking with 40 Years of Neoliberalism	108
18.	#TaxTheRich	110
19.	Rebuilding a Middle Class Gutted by Neoliberalism	111
20.	Trade: Returning to Alexander Hamilton's American Plan	117
21.	What Is Real Wealth?	123
22.	Hamilton's 11-Step Plan Worked for 188 Years	125
23.	Tariffs Built America	127
24.	But What About the Cost of American-Made Goods?	129
25.	How China Escaped Neoliberalism	133
26.	America Adopted Neoliberalism, and All I Got Was This Made-in-China T-Shirt	136
27.	Neoliberal Trade Policy Rejected by South Korea	141
28.	Reverse Privatization of Core Government Functions	145
29.	Break Up the Monopolies	148
30.	Progressive Populism to Replace Progressive Neoliberalism	149
31.	Standing on the Edge	155
NOTES		161
ACKNOWLEDGMENTS		171
INDEX		172
ABOUT THE AUTHOR		179

FOREWORD

by Greg Palast

Milton Friedman's feet didn't touch the floor. This was the University of Chicago, 1975, and Professor Friedman was God. God sat in a chair, the little man's feet dangling, as he humiliated students who deviated in the slightest from the Gospel of Friedman, what he dubbed *neoliberalism*.

I kept my head down. Friedman didn't know I was sent to study with him and his Chicago Boys by the city's labor leadership. They wanted to know if this Friedman was as dangerous as he seemed. Friedman was the not-so-hidden hand behind the new dictatorship of Chile's Augusto Pinochet. Pinochet liked to throw dissenters out of helicopters—whatever it took to create what Friedman called "The Miracle of Chile," a radical right-wing makeover of the nation's economy.

Bless Thom Hartmann for exposing the neolib Genesis story: the "Miracle" in Chile was a con. Hartmann notes that Chile's economy went into free fall under the Chicago Boys' regime; unemployment hit 30 percent.

Hartmann's book is a beautiful history of an ugly idea: that greed is good and uncontrolled greed is better, even if it leads to mass misery.

Squeezed into this thin volume is a huge amount of "I didn't know that!" info that's both horrifying and weirdly fun. I didn't know that George W. Bush's Medicare Modernization Act of 2003 resulted in the quiet privatization of nearly half of Medicare's services. Yow!

Hartmann's most original contribution is to posit that the antidote for neoliberalism's poison is not a new New Deal, but rather Alexander Hamilton's "American Plan." In 1791, at George Washington's request, Hamilton drafted a guide for strategic tariff protection, government support for jobs and industry, government regulation of products, and direct control of banking.

Hamilton's American Plan made America rich—and China too. Hartmann dismisses the baloney that China's manufacturing boom was the result of throwing the economy into the free-market soup. Hartmann was studying in China in 1986 when Chairman Deng and Premier Zhao came down on the side of Hamilton after a two-year fight with Friedmanite economists within the Communist Party.

The losing neolibs had wanted China to take "One Big Step" and follow the Soviet Union's "shock therapy"—that is, jump straight into the freezing waters of totally rule-free markets, uncontrolled international trade, privatization of industry, and shrunken government.

We know what happened: Russia is still in shock—wages and production have shriveled, life expectancy has fallen, while China's government-guided industry now produces one-eighth of the planet's goods and services.

And the United States? As Hartmann puts it in a chapter title: "America adopted neoliberalism, and all I got was this made-in-China T-shirt."

The neolibs' useful idiot, pundit Thomas Friedman, praised deregulation as "[t]he Golden Straitjacket . . . [which] first began to be stitched together and popularized by British Prime Minister Margaret Thatcher . . . [and] was soon reinforced by Ronald Reagan."[1]

Hartmann, a happy-ending kind of guy, tells us how America can unhook the straitjacket, tear off the T-shirt, and escape the neoliberal madhouse.

That's quite a feat in 192 pages.

Greg Palast, an economist turned investigative reporter, is coauthor of *Democracy and Regulation* and *The Best Democracy Money Can Buy*

The Plot to Save the World

Back in 1938, a group of economists and philosophers met in Paris to consider how to save the world from itself.[1] At the time, Mussolini, Hitler, and Franco were turning their nations into fascist concentration camps, while in Russia Stalin was killing millions of citizens he considered disloyal or unreliable, using everything from famine and gulags to firing squads.

After those three European democracies had gone full fascist, and Russia had bypassed democracy altogether to embrace a tyrannical form of communism, the Paris delegates were understandably worried about the future of democratic governance both in Europe and around the world. And the rise of communism and fascism had impacted every one of their lives personally.

The promise of fascism had been "law and order," while the promise of communism had been "no more hunger and want; all needs are met." Neither had lived up to its promise. And in both cases, economics were at the core of the systems.

Fascist governments embraced their largest corporations so tightly that Mussolini had functionally replaced most of the

Italian Parliament with representatives of his "fascist corporations."[2] The fascist theory was that when the business and government sectors operated in lockstep, they'd bring along the people with them.

The Soviet Union, on the other hand, rejected corporate control or even participation altogether, banning corporations outright. The government controlled every sector of the economy, the theory being that when government provided housing, education, and jobs, they'd bring the people along with them.

In both cases, though, the main outcome for "the people" was a loss of freedom and general misery.

How, these men who'd gathered in Paris asked, could modern democratic government be reinvented so that it wouldn't be so vulnerable to flipping either fascist or communist? How could a utopian society be created where everybody (or nearly everybody) had maximum freedom, maximum prosperity, and maximum control over their own lives?

And was it possible that economics could be the force that drove the process? Marx, after all, was an economist, as were Mussolini's main advisers. Who better than economists to invent the world anew?

The idea that the Paris group came up with was straightforward and comprised three main parts.

First, they believed that markets were both accurate and largely infallible: billions of tiny decisions were made in the marketplace of a country every day as consumers and businesses chose which products to buy or sell and which vendors to buy them from or sell them to. There was no way any group of government bureaucrats could second-guess that sort of data/computing horsepower, and, indeed, they believed that the experience of the Soviet Union, which had shattered and then outlawed markets, proved them right.

So, they reasoned, markets should drive everything possible in a society for that society to work with maximum efficiency and the best possible outcomes. Literally everything. Market logic should drive business, of course, with profit being the determiner of winners and losers, but that same market logic should drive decisions in government and even within families.

Second, they believed that democracy was inherently dangerous and needed to be constrained. In a democracy, there was always the risk that the people would vote to disrupt the healthy, normal, near-magic economic order that would result from a "free market."

The people might, essentially, vote to take wealth from the rich and give it to themselves; this would disrupt markets so badly that it would render them senseless. Indeed, the Paris economists believed that was exactly what had happened with National Socialism, or Nazism, which relied heavily on a free national single-payer health care system and free education for its support among the populace. Democracy had been too strong in those countries: it led them straight to fascism.

So instead of legislators sitting around and making their best guesses about how society should run, their main job should be to simply get out of the way so that the magical marketplace could drive all the major decisions. Democracy was fine when it came to deploying armies and police forces, or courts to adjudicate business disputes, but it needed to be blocked from interfering in moving income or wealth in any way not dictated by the marketplace.

Market forces driving all political decisions would, the Paris group believed, even end war. If governments were converted from active agents of the will of their people into passive vessels for capitalism to do its magic, the countries of the world would be so busy trading with each other that they'd never want to destroy everything with warfare.

Third, these idealists had an answer for the inevitable question: *If the government isn't going to decide what's legal and what's not, what's acceptable behavior in both the marketplace and the public square, then who should?*

If democracy were to be so hobbled that it could no longer "interfere" in the normal and healthy functioning of a nation, what would replace it as the arbiter of right and wrong?

Their answer was straightforward. Humans, they believed, had developed—over thousands of years of trial and error—a natural "moral order" with its own set of rules. Everybody, for example, knew that it was wrong to steal and wrong to kill.

So instead of regulating businesses so that they or their executives couldn't steal from or kill their customers or workers, let the free marketplace just single out, shame, and make examples of them when they did.

As thefts or deaths were exposed by a free press (part of a free market), companies committing those thefts or selling deadly products or running deadly workplaces would be abandoned by peers and customers and wither away. The moral order would be self-regulating, they said, so long as it wasn't interfered with by government.

The evolutionary process that produced strong moral codes within society couldn't be denied or resisted just because of passing moral fads.

If women had been subordinate to men for a thousand years, then that must be what was right and good and should be celebrated. If racial segregation or shunning of homosexuality was the result of a thousand years of cultural evolution, those must be the standards by which a society was strongest and most resilient, even if it offended a few people. Their era's misinterpretation of Darwin was right, even about ideas: only the strong survive.

These three principles came together neatly, these men believed.

Instead of governments running the core life of a nation, markets would do so through their participants in the marketplace, nimbly responding to a million inputs a second.

Instead of voters determining how wealth would be given, taken, or redistributed, the marketplace would make all those decisions in a way completely independent of (and often in defiance of) voters and legislators.

And instead of legislators determining what the moral code of society would be, we'd look to the past to see what had always worked and carry that forward.

Much as Marx had done with communism and Mussolini had done with fascism, the Paris group wrapped their ideas for a new utopia together in a single package and gave it a name: *neoliberalism*.

This book is the story of these men and their new form of governance, which rocked the world in the 1970s and remade most advanced democracies by the beginning of the 21st century.

And now neoliberalism, by giving outsized political power to the wealthiest among us and their industries (particularly fossil fuels), threatens to plunge the planet into a disastrous hellscape if the monster they created isn't tamed or caged.

CHAPTER 1

Save Us from the Utopians

*It may be said that effective and rational economic policies
can be implemented only by a superior leader of the
philosopher-statesman type under a powerful autocracy.*

—F. A. Hayek

Every generation has its believers in utopia, from Plato's mythical city of Magnesia[1] to Thomas More's 16th-century island of Utopia[2] to the "scientific socialism" of Karl Marx and Friedrich Engels.

Somehow, none of them worked out: Plato held slaves and was, according to Karl Popper, an early architect of multiple forms of totalitarianism (citing his influence on a particularly brutal form of early Christianity);[3] Thomas More supervised the burning alive of six Protestants and tortured a man in More's own home; Marxism's victims in the Soviet Union, East Germany, and China (among others) are well-known.

When I lived in Germany in the 1980s, I became close friends with a number of former Nazis, then in their late-middle years, who'd followed Hitler in their youth (most were in their teens when the war ended) because he'd promised to bring the world "a thousand years of peace" and worldwide harmony through National Socialism.[4]

In the early 1980s, my wife, Louise, and I spent a few weeks on a small sailing ship off the coast of Malaysia with Dr. Will Krynen, who'd worked for the Red Cross and treated Pol Pot as he was dying in Cambodia.[5] Pol Pot had reset the calendar to "Year Zero" in 1975[6] and overseen the murders of over a million Cambodians whose crime was that they were literate—because he was convinced that people who knew nothing of history were a blank slate on which an entire new, utopian society could be written.

The idea wasn't unique to Pol Pot.

Borrowing revolutionary fervor from the Jeffersonians, Maximilien Robespierre declared 1793 as Year One of the First French Republic, which he kicked off in September 1792. He even renamed the months of the year in a break with France's Catholic/Roman calendar past. Mirabeau, Marat, Danton, Robespierre, and other members of the Committee of Public Safety truly believed they could create a paradise on Earth if they just got rid of France's royal and feudal past, chopped the heads off 1,376 people, and, essentially, started over from scratch.

That idea was so appealing to Russia's Bolsheviks that in 1918, they too dumped the Julian calendar.[7] In November of that year, in Alexander's Garden (now under the walls of the Kremlin), they erected a monument to Robespierre commissioned by Vladimir Lenin himself (another leader who promised utopia).[8] A road named Quai Robespierre carries the French revolutionary's memory in Moscow.

Here in America, we were somewhat less extreme in our revolution, although we did evict the British (killing tens of thousands) and began an experiment with republican democracy that had largely lain fallow for several thousand years. In the early years of the George Washington presidency, his Treasury secretary, Alexander Hamilton, put into place what he called the American Plan, which succeeded in producing what was then the world's greatest explosion of wealth and the first American middle class (more about that later).

Almost 80 years after the American Revolution, the American Civil War could be cast as a battle between two competing utopian ideals: democracy in the North and a slavery-based oligarchy in the South (as I detail at length in *The Hidden History of American Oligarchy: Reclaiming Our Democracy from the Ruling Class*). The Confederate revolutionaries lost their quest to remodel all of America after the late-stage slaveholding Roman Republic (although their heirs continue the fight).

The next American revolution came in the 1930s, when President Franklin D. Roosevelt won his effort to overhaul America's economic and political system, ending the Republican Great Depression and helping our allies end fascism in Japan, Italy, and Germany (it continued in Spain until the 1970s).

And FDR's reinvention of America did, indeed and finally, produce widespread prosperity, a massive expansion of democracy, and the largest and fastest-growing middle class in the history of the world to that point.

But every revolution has its counterrevolutionaries; Confederates had attacked the heirs of Washington's revolution and failed; American oligarchs went after Roosevelt in the early 1930s, even attempting to kidnap or kill him in the so-called Business Plot.

But by the late 1970s, a far deeper and more widespread counterrevolution against FDR's New Deal had begun to take root, first in the United Kingdom with the 1979 election of Margaret Thatcher as Great Britain's prime minister and then in the United States with the 1980 election of Ronald Reagan as president.

By that time, it wasn't Lindbergh's Nazi sympathizers and America Firsters who took on and then largely took down FDR's Keynesian revolution: it was the American followers of two Austrian economists and an American academic from the University of Chicago who was, on the side, secretly hustling for the real estate industry.

Friedrich August von Hayek (more commonly known as F. A. Hayek), Ludwig von Mises, Milton Friedman, and their followers truly believed that FDR's revolution—and the reconfiguration of economies across Europe using his Keynesian economic model—would end in disaster, something close to the Soviet takeover of Russia or even Hitler's rise in Germany, and so they launched their own counterrevolution.

To stop the dangers of FDR's Keynesian economics and its widespread popularity across America and around the world, they said it was vital to privatize government functions, radically cut taxes on rich people and big corporations while imposing "austerity" on everybody else, and eliminate national policies that protected labor (from tariffs to unions) by creating a single global marketplace.

That movement, which they called *neoliberalism* and which, in America, is sometimes known as Reaganomics or the Third Way (a movement that came out of President Bill Clinton's neoliberal New Democrat Caucus and that showed up in the UK as Tony Blair's New Labor), was supposed to set aside the trappings and powers of government to allow the free market to reshape everything from the world economy to each nation's federal government to the world's families.

It would, they fervently believed, use the magic of the market to bring widespread prosperity, increase freedom, and ultimately stabilize politics in messy democracies worldwide.

Instead, their neoliberal movement reshaped the American political and economic landscape in ways the neoliberal evangelists failed to initially foresee (but later, particularly in Chile and Russia, embraced), leading to political violence, widespread poverty, massive inequality, and a political backlash that included the election of Donald Trump and led to this era's crisis of democracy.

Today the neoliberal movement has seized control of much of the developed world and, at the same time, is fighting for its life as the depth and breadth of its disaster is increasingly recognized across the world.

Between the election of America's first neoliberal president, Ronald Reagan, and 2019, household income going to the top 1 percent of Americans doubled, while the bottom 90 percent saw no meaningful increase in income at all.[9]

CEO pay went up by almost a thousand percent, as the richest 0.1 percent of Americans saw their wealth rise from 10 percent of all the wealth in America in 1980 to over 20 percent by 2020, more than the combined wealth of the entire bottom *half* of American families, who today own a mere 1.3 percent of this nation's wealth.[10]

Meanwhile, the richest Americans have captured our political system: the richest one-hundredth of 1 percent of Americans made over 40 percent of all campaign contributions in 2016, while corporations poured $3.4 *billion* into the 2016 election after moving more than 60,000 factories overseas.[11]

Increasingly, Americans are aware of these trends—entirely traceable back to neoliberal policies put into place in the 1980s and holding until 2021—and are pissed off about it.

The result of neoliberalism's dramatic failure in the United States is that Americans are, once again, on the edge of another generational revolution, both political and economic. Similar movements against neoliberalism are rising across the developed and developing world, some in ways that could be so destabilizing as to lead to a third world war.

CHAPTER 2

The Birth of
Neoliberalism

A field of battle covered with dead bodies putrefying in the open air is an awful and distressing spectacle, but a nation debased by the love of money and exhibiting all the vices and crimes usually connected with that passion, is a spectacle far more awful, distressing and offensive.

—Letter from Dr. Benjamin Rush to Thomas Jefferson, 1813

The past 3,000 years have seen the emergence of several great forces that have shaped the modern world: the nation-state, feudalism, capitalism, democracy, and, most recently, communism and neoliberalism.

Since the widespread adoption of agriculture and the subsequent increase in available food, and the steadily rising population that came along with it, nation-states emerged around the world, starting in a big way around 3,000 years ago, from the Maya and Aztecs to the kingdoms of Europe and Asia to the caliphates of the Middle East and the Bantu takeover of much of Africa.[1]

Various forms of feudalism emerged with most nation-states: power was seized by those willing to engage in violence to gain control of land and the food supply it produced, as well as other early forms of wealth.

These early kings (known by many other names and titles) claimed that they owned not only the land that made up their nation-states but also the people upon them. They forced young men into their armies, had their way with their choice of young women (some kings having harems of hundreds), and demanded tributes or taxes of a share of each serf's productivity (typically part of the food they grew).

As economies became increasingly complex and sophisticated, early forms of capitalism emerged, complete with the debt peonage and rapid, multigenerational accumulations of wealth by a small percentage of the people. These primary characteristics—widespread debt and massive economic (and thus political power) inequality—continue to this day as both hallmarks of capitalism and problems in creating functioning societies.

The earliest forms of writing—clay tablets and cuneiform alphabets—were most commonly used to record commercial transactions and debt; such bookkeeping relics dating back as much as 4,000 years ago, the earliest from the Middle East and Asia, are today proudly displayed in museums around the world.

Those who had wealth—today we'd call it capital—used it to employ those without wealth to help the wealthy increase their own wealth while sharing a small slice with their employees or using some of it to feed and house those whom they'd seized against their will or who were simply in debt peonage.

Today we call this system *free-market capitalism*: slavery, dynastic fortunes, and monopolies were its foundation. Philosophers, economists, and leaders from Aristotle to Adam

Smith, Karl Marx to Franklin D. Roosevelt, struggled to find ways to make capitalism produce prosperity while minimizing its deleterious effects.

Three thousand years ago, the people of Greek nation-states (principally Athens) began experimenting with a form of governance that harked back to and imitated many of the aspects of the (usually) egalitarian tribal governance that marked human societies for at least the past 60,000 years. They called it *democracy*, from the Greek words for *people* and *rule*.

To call any of these systems purely economic or purely governmental/political is a mistake; wealth and governance have been intertwined ever since the first emergence of agricultural settlements seven millennia ago.

Thus, we "modern" postagricultural humans have always struggled to forge political solutions to economic injustices, particularly the problems inherent in feudalism and capitalism.

For example, while Adam Smith's 1776 book *The Wealth of Nations* is well known and widely quoted (particularly the single reference to the "invisible hand" of the marketplace that is almost always quoted out of context), he believed that his far more important contribution to the field of economics was his 1759 book *The Theory of Moral Sentiments*, which outlined ways capitalism might be regulated to minimize its "moral" harms.

Marx similarly struggled with how to minimize capitalism's harms, most famously in his 1867 three-volume work (which he completed in 1883), *Das Kapital*. His diagnosis of the problems intrinsic to capitalism has largely stood the test of time, but his solution—to do away with capitalism altogether and have all economic and political issues handled by the state—

hasn't worked out as well in practice as he and his followers believed it would. In fact, it's been a disaster every time it's been put into place on a large scale.

Marxists, of course, would argue that the problem with communism is that it hasn't really been tried, pointing to Israeli kibbutzim, Jesus and his disciples' "common purse," and various communal experiments around the world as examples of its ancestry and possibilities.

Similarly, ideological proponents of capitalism argue that it hasn't truly been tried either, at least in the modern nation-state. The more the state tries to regulate capitalism to reduce its harms, they say, the more the state distorts it as a system and produces the very problems it claims to be solving.

It's out of this last debate that neoliberalism emerged in the mid-20th century. Like Marx rejecting capitalism altogether, neoliberals reject the regulation of capitalism by the state in any meaningful way.

As F. A. Hayek wrote in Volume 2 (1976) of *Law, Legislation and Liberty*:

> *The more dependent the position of the individuals or groups is seen to become on the actions of government, the more they will insist that the governments aim at some recognizable scheme of distributive justice; and the more governments try to realize some preconceived pattern of desirable distribution, the more they must subject the position of the different individuals and groups to their control. So long as the belief in "social justice" governs political action, this process must progressively approach nearer and nearer to a totalitarian system.*[2]

The word *neoliberalism* was coined by a group of economists that included the Austrians Ludwig von Mises and F. A. Hayek, who first got together in Paris in 1938 at a dinner honoring Walter Lippmann.

The term was later popularized by the Mont Pelerin Society, which still exists and grew out of a 1947 meeting at Hayek's invitation at a hotel on Mont Pelerin (*Mount* Pelerin in English) in Vevey on Lac Léman (also known as Lake Geneva), Switzerland, shortly after the end of World War II.[3]

The majority of the 39 attendees at Hayek's April 1, 1947, meeting were economists, most famously Ludwig von Mises and Milton Friedman, although there were a few historians and philosophers who shared the group's skepticism of government intervention in markets. They came from Germany, Switzerland, France, England, Norway, Italy, and the United States.[4]

They added the prefix *neo*, meaning "new" in Greek (*néos*), to *liberalism*, a word that to this day is used by Europeans to describe what we in America would call *laissez-faire* or largely unregulated capitalism. (What Americans call *liberalism* most Europeans would call *democratic socialism* or *social democracy*.)

These white men (all were men) believed that in the duel between capitalism and democracy, capitalism must always be in a superior position of power; most argued that democracy —which their followers often refer to as "mob rule"—is an absolutely inferior way to govern a nation. Just leave everything to the magical marketplace and the billionaires who own and manage most of it, and everything will work out just fine.

At the end of the meeting, they issued a "Statement of Aims" that opened with alarm: "The central values of civilization are in danger. . . . Even that most precious possession of

Western Man, freedom of thought and expression, is threatened by the spread of creeds which, claiming the privilege of tolerance when in the position of a minority, seek only to establish a position of power in which they can suppress and obliterate all views but their own."[5]

The statement called for "[t]he redefinition of the functions of the state so as to distinguish more clearly between the totalitarian and the liberal order."[6]

In other words, the "creeds" of the modern democracies of the 1940s that were expanding government services like free health care and education for working-class people threatened to destroy "freedom of thought and expression" and could only lead to totalitarianism.

To this day, they hold that line, a complete inversion of Abraham Lincoln's expression of centuries of American conventional wisdom, which he laid out in his 1861 State of the Union address: "Labor is prior to and independent of capital. Capital is only the fruit of labor, and could never have existed if labor had not first existed. Labor is the superior of capital, and deserves much the higher consideration."[7]

When I asked economist Stephen Moore, of the Heritage Foundation and the Reagan and Trump administrations, to tell me on my radio program which was more important, capitalism or democracy, he immediately responded, "Capitalism, of course!"[8]

The weakness and corruptibility of democracy is constantly cited by Rand Paul libertarians, Ayn Rand objectivists, and neoliberals like Moore as one of the reasons why the magical marketplace and its billionaires should be running America (and the world) rather than "the mob."

CHAPTER 3

Neoliberalism's Fathers: Mises, Hayek, and Friedman

Few discoveries are more irritating than those which expose the pedigree of ideas.

—Lord Acton[1]

Ludwig von Mises and the "Critical Race Theory" of Neoliberalism

To say that Ludwig von Mises and F. A. Hayek were both traumatized and influenced by their respective brushes with Nazism would be an understatement.

Mises suffered the indignity of Hitler's Gestapo seizing 21 boxes of his papers and taking over his apartment in March 1938. Two years later, he fled to the United States, where, ironically, he advocated many of Hitler's racial ideas and even integrated them into his economic ideology. "It must be emphasized," he wrote, "that the destiny of modern civilization as developed by the white peoples in the last two hundred years is inseparably linked with the fate of economic science."[2]

He thought Hitler was a passing fad and wrote that because of the racial composition of Germany, "Fascists carry on their work among nations in which the intellectual and moral heritage of some thousands of years of civilization cannot be destroyed at one blow, and not among the barbarian [Slavic and Asiatic] peoples on both sides of the Urals, whose relationship to civilization has never been any other than that of marauding denizens of forest and desert accustomed to engage, from time to time, in predatory raids on civilized lands in the hunt for booty."[3]

The excesses of Hitler, Mises believed, were merely an understandable response to the horrors of Soviet Communism committed by the inferior Slavic peoples and would, in Germany, eventually moderate into a free-market system.

"The deeds of the Fascists and of other parties corresponding to them," he wrote, "were emotional reflex actions evoked by indignation at the deeds of the Bolsheviks and Communists. As soon as the first flush of anger had passed, their policy took a more moderate course and will probably become even more so with the passage of time."[4]

Mises preached that it was the obligation of the superior races of Europe to, essentially, civilize inferior races all around the world, while retaining their own racial purity. The intelligence and abilities of people weren't found in how they grew up; it was all in their genes. We're born how we are, he believed, not made that way by our life's experiences.

He wrote, "The influence of environment is estimated to be low: mixture of races creates bastards, in whom the good hereditary qualities of the nobler races deteriorate or are lost. . . . [C]ertain influences, operating over a long period, have bred one race or several, with specially favourable qualities, and the members of these races had by means of these advantages obtained so long a lead that members of other races could not overtake them within a limited time."

This justified the white civilized people of the world not only helping out the inferior people but also putting them to work!

"We see at once that it [race theory] contains nothing directly inimical to the doctrine of the division of labour," he wrote. "The two are quite compatible. It may be assumed that races do differ in intelligence and will power, and that, this being so, they are very unequal in their ability to form society, and further that the better races distinguish themselves precisely by their special aptitude for strengthening social co-operation."[5]

As if he'd just said or discovered something particularly profound, Mises's next two sentences put a punctuation mark on his justification for white neoliberal imperialism: "This hypothesis throws light on various aspects of social evolution not otherwise easily comprehensible. It enables us to explain the development and regression of the social division of labour and the flowering and decline of civilizations."

Thus, "free trade" would be a blessing to the world even if it involved exploiting what he considered inferior people: "When the race theory combats the natural law postulate of the equality and equal rights of all men, it does not affect the free trade argument. . . . In the race theory there are no arguments to refute free trade theory as to the effects of the expanding social division of labour. It may be admitted that the races differ in talent and character and that there is no hope of ever seeing those differences resolved."[6]

Acknowledging this simple reality, Mises wrote, would liberate the world via neoliberalism while raising up the "less capable" races, who would now be given the privilege of laboring for the "more capable" races and thus learning techniques that would increase their productivity: "Still, free trade theory shows that even the more capable races derive an advantage from associating with the less capable and that social co-operation brings them the advantage of higher productivity in the total labour process."[7]

Mises's theory that neoliberal "free trade" would conquer the world and the "more capable" races would, like the statue of Colossus, ride astride that one world market applied both to Black and Asian people. And it would be their salvation!

"If the Asiatics and Africans," he wrote, "really enter into the orbit of Western civilization, they will have to adopt the market economy without reservations."[8] Hitler and the men who ransacked Mises's apartment would have smiled; they were saying pretty much the same thing.

F. A. Hayek vs. the Birth of Democratic Socialism

Friedrich August von Hayek studied at the knee of Mises during what Mises called his "private seminars" in the offices of the Vienna Chamber of Commerce on that city's Ringstrasse (Grand Boulevard) between 1920 and 1934. Out of this developed a lifelong friendship, the formation of the Mont Pelerin Society, and the new economic religion of neoliberalism.

By 1940, the year Mises emigrated to the United States, Hayek had also fled the Nazis, although he'd moved to London (he became a British citizen in 1938), which was then being regularly bombed by Hitler's Luftwaffe. As the bombing campaign, the Blitz, became more aggressive that year, Hayek began to seriously worry about the possibility that a bomb could kill his children.

This was a turning point for his family, and he thought that America, daily becoming more egalitarian and leading the world out of the Republican Great Depression with FDR's New Deal, would offer them the best opportunities.

Hayek hoped that instead of being inculcated with the ancient social and royal hierarchies of Europe, they would learn—as long as they were living with white Americans—a more modern, socially conscious, and civilized way of living. "For the sake of my children who still had to develop their personalities," Hayek wrote, "I felt that the very absence in the USA of the sharp social distinctions which would favour me in the Old World should make me decide for them in favour of the former."[9] He continued, parenthetically, "I should perhaps add that this was based on the tacit assumption that my children would there be placed with a white and not with a coloured family."

His seminal and most famous book, *The Road to Serfdom*, was published without much fanfare in the UK in 1944, but the following year it came out in an American edition and made a huge splash among the growing neoliberal-movement economists and even large parts of the conservative general public. (He followed his children to the United States in 1950.)

Reading *The Road to Serfdom* is like stepping into a political and cultural time machine.

Unlike his mentor Mises, who wrote in his book *Socialism*, "The foremost demands of the national-socialist [Nazi] agitation are different from those of the Marxists,"[10] Hayek believed that the biggest challenge facing the world wasn't a creeping welfare state that would inevitably lead to *communism* but, instead, that a creeping welfare state would put the UK and US on the same path that Hitler trod to *fascism*.

Germany's social welfare state was the first among all other developed nations by the end of the 1920s, that country having led the pack by initiating the world's first single-payer health care system in 1884 and expanded later on Social Security–like pension systems.[11]

Following Germany's defeat in World War I, the kaiser stepped down in 1918, the Weimar Republic was born in 1919, and by 1927 that country had put into place a new constitution; laws protecting the rights of labor (leading to a steady rise in wages and growth of a middle class, peaking in 1928 with a 10 percent rise in wages just that year); national "pension and sickness benefit schemes" (what we'd call Social Security and paid family and sickness leave); a massive program building low-income housing, schools, parks, and hospitals; and a national program of unemployment insurance (1927).[12]

This German abandonment of free-market hands-off government and embrace of a modern social safety net was, Hayek believed, the *cause* of Hitlerism and the Nazi movement that had forced him and his family out of Europe. And if the US and the UK continued down the road that the Germans had taken in the 1920s, he was convinced, we were doomed to confront an American version of Germany's terrible experience.

"It is necessary now to state the unpalatable truth that it is Germany whose fate we are in some danger of repeating," he wrote. "Few are ready to recognize that the rise of fascism and naziism was not a reaction against the social trends of the preceding period but a necessary outcome of those tendencies."[13]

There's an important distinction between the Soviet system and the German welfare state of the 1920s, which was more like the American welfare state of the post-1933 New Deal and the British welfare state that emerged with the end of World War II. The Soviets had taken to heart Marx's admonition that the *means of production* must be owned by the state, along with caring for the people's needs.

Every industry in the USSR, from making cars, blue jeans, and steel, to publishing books, building houses, and even making pharmaceuticals had been taken over by the Soviet government, which became the entire nation's sole employer. The Soviet government was unmistakably communist.

But in Germany, the United Kingdom, and the United States, outside of natural monopolies like utilities, schools, and police/fire, all production and employment was still in private hands. The government regulated industry to protect workers from exploitation, protect consumers from dangerous or poisonous products, and keep the air and water clean, but didn't own any major industries.

And Germany under Hitler's Nazi government not only did *not* nationalize industries as the Soviets had done, but— as Prime Minister Margaret Thatcher would do in the UK— undertook a widespread *privatization* program, turning previously government-owned or -run parts of the "steel, mining, banking, shipyard, ship-lines, and railways" over *entirely* to the private sector.[14]

That reality, however, didn't deter Mises and Hayek from their certainty about the dangers of a strong social safety net in democratic republics like the US and the UK.

While Mises had looked at the social welfare systems of all three countries (US, UK, Germany) and saw them leading to Soviet-style communism and race-mixing, Hayek saw in programs like unemployment insurance and low-income housing subsidies the seeds of a new Nazism.

And he was extremely frustrated that it wasn't obvious on its face to the citizens of the US and the UK.

"It seems almost as if we do not want to understand the development which has produced totalitarianism," he wrote in *The Road to Serfdom*, "because such an understanding might destroy some of the dearest illusions to which we are determined to cling."[15]

Hayek wrote of how "many of my Anglo-Saxon friends have sometimes been shocked by the semi-Fascist views they would occasionally hear expressed by German refugees," but this, he said, wasn't caused by their being exposed to Hitler's ideas for a decade.

"[T]he true explanation," he wrote of the fascist-friendly German refugees, "is that they were socialists whose experience had carried them several stages beyond that yet reached by socialists in England and America."

They were still sympathetic in some ways to the fascists, in other words, because Germany had a *more comprehensive* "Prussian" social safety net than did the UK or US, and these refugees "favored" their unemployment insurance, Social Security system, and single-payer health care.

"It was the prevalence of socialist views and not Prussianism," Hayek wrote, "that Germany had in common with Italy and Russia—and it was from the masses and not the classes steeped in the Prussian tradition, and favored by it, that National Socialism [Nazism] arose."[16]

Weirdly, this inversion of reality has taken hold in the contemporary American right. Sen. Rand Paul (R-KY) wrote in his 2019 book *The Case Against Socialism* that the simple reality is that "Hitler was a socialist."[17]

Paul went on to suggest that because Germany was a welfare state when Hitler rose to power and stayed that way (at least for loyal or nonpolitical "Aryans") through Hitler's reign, Adolf Hitler had to have been a hard-core socialist.

The word *socialism* in *National Socialism* (abbreviated to *Nazi*) was, in reality, just Hitler affirming that he wanted white Aryans—and only white Aryans—to continue to have a social safety net and worker protections in place. From an interview with the *American Monthly* magazine in 1923:

"Why," I asked Hitler, "do you call yourself a National Socialist, since your party programme is the very antithesis of that commonly accredited to socialism?"

"Socialism," he retorted, putting down his cup of tea, pugnaciously, "is the science of dealing with the common weal. Communism is not Socialism. Marxism is not Socialism. The Marxians have stolen the term and confused its meaning. I shall take Socialism away from the Socialists.

"Socialism is an ancient Aryan, Germanic institution. Our German ancestors held certain lands in common. They cultivated the idea of the common weal. Marxism has no

right to disguise itself as socialism. Socialism, unlike Marx-
ism, does not repudiate private property. Unlike Marxism,
it involves no negation of personality, and unlike Marxism,
it is patriotic.

"We might have called ourselves the Liberal Party. We
chose to call ourselves the National Socialists. We are not inter-
nationalists. Our socialism is national. We demand the fulfil-
ment of the just claims of the productive classes by the state on
the basis of race solidarity. To us state and race are one."[18]

Bizarrely, both Hayek and Paul ignore the fact that Hitler waged an internal war against the *actual* socialists (pretty
much no matter how you define the word) in Germany.

On March 23, 1933, Hitler pushed the Enabling Acts
through the Reichstag and the following week arrested all 81
elected Communist and 26 of the 120 elected Social Democrat members of Parliament; he sent all of them to concentration camps, and virtually all of the hundreds of thousands of
members of both parties were either sent to camps to die or
blocked from employment for the rest of his reign.[19]

But a simple online search of the words "Hitler" and
"socialism" will find literally thousands of web pages devoted
to arguing Paul's and Hayek's view that Hitler had, in modern
economic and political terms, more in common with Bernie
Sanders than with Pol Pot.

Hayek laid out this bizarre theory, now almost fully
embraced by the American right, unambiguously in *The Road
to Serfdom*:

Although most of the new ideas, and particularly socialism, did not originate in Germany, it was in Germany that they were perfected and during the last quarter of the nineteenth and the first quarter of the twentieth century that they reached their fullest development. It is now often forgotten how very considerable was the lead which Germany had during this period in the development of the theory and practice of socialism; that a generation before socialism became a serious issue in this country [the UK], Germany had a large socialist party in her parliament and that until not very long ago the doctrinal development of socialism was almost entirely carried out in Germany and Austria, so that even today Russian discussion largely carries on where the Germans left off. Most English and American socialists are still unaware that the majority of the problems they began to discover were thoroughly discussed by German socialists long ago.[20]

That most Americans and Brits don't consider themselves either Nazis or socialists, and believe *capitalism* is the core economic system of both countries, is, according to Hayek, purely a function of the amazingly effective propaganda employed by those wily socialists.

"To make a totalitarian system function efficiently," Hayek wrote, "it is not enough that everybody should be forced to work for the same ends. It is essential that the people should come to regard them as their own ends. Although the beliefs must be chosen for the people and imposed upon them, they must become their beliefs. . . . This is, of course, brought about by the various forms of propaganda. Its technique is now so familiar that we need say little about it."[21]

Milton Friedman

The American among the Three Musketeers of neoliberalism was Milton Friedman, who taught for years at the Chicago School of Economics and has become a figure of cult worship on the economic and political right in America.

He was a speechwriter for Barry Goldwater's 1960 campaign for president and a formal adviser to, among others, Richard Nixon, Ronald Reagan, Margaret Thatcher, and Donald Rumsfeld (whom Friedman pushed Reagan to take on as his VP instead of GHW Bush in 1980).[22]

Friedman was the functional theologian among the three; he absolutely believed that there was a near-mystical power to unregulated markets and that virtually any sort of governmental intervention in or regulation of the marketplace produced economic distortions that prevented capitalism from working its magic.

When, in his first inaugural address on January 20, 1981, President Reagan said, "Government is not the solution to our problem, government *is* the problem," he was merely echoing Friedman.[23]

Twenty years earlier, Friedman had watched John F. Kennedy give his inaugural address and cringed when Kennedy hit his most memorable high point:

In the long history of the world, only a few generations have been granted the role of defending freedom in its hour of maximum danger. I do not shrink from this responsibility—I welcome it. I do not believe that any of us would exchange places with any other people or any other generation. The energy, the faith, the devotion which we bring to this endeavor will light our country and all who serve it— and the glow from that fire can truly light the world.

And so, my fellow Americans: ask not what your country can do for you—ask what you can do for your country.[24]

Kennedy's speech sent Friedman into such a paroxysm of fury that he opened his 1962 book *Capitalism and Freedom* by attacking it on page one.

In a much quoted passage in his inaugural address, President Kennedy said, "Ask not what your country can do for you—ask what you can do for your country."

Neither half of the statement expresses a relation between the citizen and his government that is worthy of the ideals of free men in a free society. The paternalistic "what your country can do for you" implies that government is the patron, the citizen the ward, a view that is at odds with the free man's belief in his own responsibility for his own destiny. The organismic, "what you can do for your country" implies the government is the master or the deity, the citizen, the servant or the votary.[25]

Friedman's devotee Margaret Thatcher famously told *Women's Own* magazine in 1987, "And, you know, there is no such thing as society. There are individual men and women, and there are families, and no government can do anything except through people, and people must look to themselves first."[26]

She got it from Friedman's 1962 book *Capitalism and Freedom*, whose next sentence after his anti-Kennedy rant was, "To the free man, the country is the collection of individuals who compose it, not something over and above them."

If it sounds like they're both echoing President Thomas Jefferson in saying that a government should only function by "the consent of the governed,"[27] they very much are not.

If the "governed" want a social safety net, for example, or want Social Security, a national health care system, or unemployment insurance, Friedman, Thatcher, and today's American Republican Party argue, that is something they should be denied because it will lead to communism (Mises and Friedman) or Nazism (Hayek).

Neoliberalism, instead, explicitly demands a "free market" system where all social needs are met by the magical marketplace and the morbidly rich who control it, rather than by people banding together and taxing themselves to provide such benefits through government. No matter what percentage of the population likes those "free" things, they all lead, neoliberals will tell you, to bondage.

As Friedman wrote in the paragraph following his anti-Kennedy rant, "The free man will ask neither what his country can do for him *nor* what he can do for his country."

Even the kinds of basic government regulation that most people want will destroy freedom, Friedman argued, saying, for example, that licensing doctors to practice medicine is a step too far.

In his chapter titled "Occupational Licensure," Friedman wrote, "The medical profession is one in which practice of the profession has for a long time been restricted to people with licenses. Offhand, the question, 'Ought we to let incompetent physicians practice?' seems to admit of only a negative answer. But I want to urge that second thought may give pause."

He went on to rant about how licensure is about protecting not the public but greedy elites trying to prevent "free people" from doing whatever they want while keeping the income for doctors high. This applies, Friedman said, to everything from plumbers' unions to the AMA.

"The American Medical Association is perhaps the strongest trade union in the United States," he wrote. "The essence of the power of a trade union is its power to restrict the number who may engage in a particular occupation. This restriction may be exercised indirectly by being able to enforce a wage rate higher than would otherwise prevail. If such a wage rate can be enforced, it will reduce the number of people who can get jobs and thus indirectly the number of people pursuing the occupation. . . . [T]he American Medical Association is in this position."[28]

And if there was anything that Milton Friedman wanted to destroy, it was trade unions and the government regulation that made it possible for them to legally withstand often-violent assaults from employers.

Along those same lines, in 1946 Friedman got into (metaphorical) bed with Herbert Nelson, "the chief lobbyist and executive vice president for the National Association of Real Estate Boards, and one of the highest paid lobbyists in the nation," as well as a cofounder of the Foundation for Economic Education (FEE), which invented the Libertarian Party as a political rationale to deregulate the real estate industry.[29]

No fan of actual government, at least as understood by most Americans, Nelson famously said, "I do not believe in democracy. I think it stinks. I don't think anybody except direct taxpayers should be allowed to vote. I don't believe women should be allowed to vote at all. Ever since they started, our public affairs have been in a worse mess than ever."[30]

Friedman cowrote a booklet for Nelson's FEE trashing the idea of rent controls titled *Roofs or Ceilings? The Current Housing Problem.*[31] FEE had amassed a multimillion-dollar war chest, according to author Mark Ames, and while the amount Friedman was paid for his work (the FEE ordered a half-million copies printed) has never been disclosed, it represented Friedman's entrée into the world of big business, which embraced him with vigor.

Friedman jumped right into the fray on behalf of big business, repeatedly arguing that when a corporation put social responsibility over profits, it was engaged in the most wicked form of socialism. Regardless of the harm to the environment, workers, society, or even democracy, any legal thing a corporation did to increase its profits was necessary to prevent collectivist communism from emerging in America.

As he wrote in the *New York Times* in 1970,

> [T]he doctrine of "social responsibility" taken seriously
> would extend the scope of the political mechanism to
> every human activity. It does not differ in philosophy from
> the most explicitly collective doctrine. It differs only by
> professing to believe that collectivist ends can be attained
> without collectivist means. That is why, in my book

Capitalism and Freedom, *I have called it a "fundamentally subversive doctrine" in a free society, and have said that in such a society, "there is one and only one social responsibility of business—to use its resources and engage in activities designed to increase its profits so long as it stays within the rules of the game, which is to say, engages in open and free competition without deception or fraud."*[32]

Friedman also believed that because most citizens of developed countries liked their governments regulating things that affected their safety and providing them with a larger social safety net, it was necessary to either use natural disasters or create crises to bring about the unpopular imposition of neoliberalism. As he wrote in the preface to the 1982 edition of *Capitalism and Freedom*, "There is an enormous inertia—the tyranny of the status quo—in private and especially government arrangements. Only a crisis—actual or perceived—produces real change. When that crisis occurs, the actions that are taken depend on the ideas that are lying around. That, I believe, is our basic function: to develop alternatives to existing policies, to keep them alive and available until the politically impossible becomes politically inevitable."

Thus was born what author Naomi Klein famously termed "The Shock Doctrine," the title of her seminal and best-selling 2007 book, laying out how giant corporations took advantage of a wide spectrum of crises, natural *and* human-made, to eliminate the socially protective functions of government and replace them with neoliberal rule by the rich and the corporate.[33]

CHAPTER 4

Neoliberalism
Goes to Work

The nation is, at this time, so strong and united in its sentiments,
that it cannot be shaken at this moment. But suppose a series of
untoward events should occur, sufficient to bring into doubt the
competency of a republican government to meet a crisis of great
danger, or to unhinge the confidence of the people in the public
functionaries; an institution like this, penetrating by its branches
every part of the Union, acting by command and in phalanx,
may, in a critical moment, upset the government.

—President Thomas Jefferson[1]

Neoliberalism has a few primary tenets that are easily identi-
fied and make it unique from libertarianism, objectivism, and
the "conservative" economic policies of the United States in
the years prior to the neoliberal Reagan Revolution of 1981.
They include the following beliefs:

- Controlling inflation is the most important job of
  federal economic regulation, and austerity (a lack
  of government participation in the lives of its people, particularly in any supportive way) is the best
  way to get there.

- National economies must be deregulated because
  the market is smarter than government agencies
  or bureaucrats.

- State-owned enterprises, from natural monopolies like city-run utilities and air-traffic control to schools and programs like Social Security and Medicare, must all be privatized; all "welfare" programs must end.

- Governments must be shrunk radically, both to decrease their power and to liberate corporations and individuals of great wealth to work their market magic.

- Taxes should be cut to the bone; if the "beast of government" can't be shrunk, it must be starved.

- Markets shouldn't be centered in or favor any particular nation: the entire world is the free-market stage on which corporations and morbidly rich capitalists must be free to work their magic.

- Property rights are more important than human rights, and racial, religious, and gender discrimination and their attendant economic inequalities are problems to be solved not by governments but by free markets and the people who dominate those marketplaces.

Out of these core tenets come a group of corollaries that, while not often articulated publicly, are the plainly visible outcome of the rapid imposition of neoliberalism. We see these behavior patterns repeated whenever neoliberalism seizes a country, whether it be modest neoliberalism as in the US and UK or "shock neoliberalism" as was imposed in Chile, Iraq, and Russia:

- Markets (capitalism) are superior to votes (democracy), so all necessary steps are justified to impose neoliberalism on "welfare state" democracies even when the majority of citizens oppose it.

- While there can be barriers to the free movement of people between nations, there should be no barriers to the corporate free trade movement of goods or money.

- Any involvement of government in the lives of its citizens outside of law enforcement and a defensive military inevitably leads to a loss of freedom for corporations and the very wealthy and therefore should be ended or privatized.

- The family is the best metaphor for governance, with a strong male leader who can overcome the inevitable resistance of what Ayn Rand (who attended a later Mont Pelerin meeting) called "the moochers," using clear lines of authority and long-established gender roles.

- The welfare state must be ended; it's inherently violent and coercive because it's paid for by taxes taken by the threat of government violence (guns, jails) from well-off people, and it also destroys incentive to work by providing for low-income people's basic needs.

- Even government functions as widely accepted as licensing physicians are inappropriate interventions in a free market (which is why Rand Paul

created his very own ophthalmologic "board" to
certify his unused medical license).

- Even fascism and oligarchy (as practiced in Chile
and Russia on the advice of Milton Friedman's
Chicago Boys neoliberals who helped reorganize
the economies of both countries) are acceptable
alternatives to welfare-state democracy.

- Competition, not cooperation, is the defining
characteristic of all truly important human inter-
actions; winners should be celebrated and losers
ignored.

- Inequality is a sign that society is working as it
should because the market rewards the most com-
petent and punishes or leaves behind those not
able or willing to carry their own weight.

- Citizenship is secondary; the citizens of a country
should instead be seen and treated as consumers
because the economy is more critical than the
state.

- Monopolies are indicators of great efficiency in
meeting the needs of the market and shouldn't be
feared or regulated.

- Labor unions impede corporate management's
ability to make unilateral decisions and thus are
antithetical to a freely functioning economy and a
free nation.

- Controlling inflation is more important than
preventing unemployment.

- Tax havens and other ways for wealthy people and corporations to avoid "paying their fair share" are an economic and social *good* because they simply reward hard work and innovation while denying resources to the beast of government.

CHAPTER 5

Worldwide Neoliberalism Experiments

*Blind faith in the efficiency of deregulated financial markets
and the absence of a cooperative financial and monetary system
created an illusion of risk-free profits and licensed profligacy
through speculative finance.*

—United Nations Conference on Trade and Development,
The Global Economic Crisis[1]

The neoliberal ideology of Mises, Hayek, and Friedman has now heavily influenced much of the developed and developing world, creating economic, political, and social disasters in countries from Thailand to South Africa to El Salvador. But its biggest openly declared national-scale experiments were kicked off in 1973 in Chile, 1981 in the United States, and 1991 in Russia.

In each case, rejecting a democratic government of, by, and for the people and replacing it with a corporatist government of, by, and for the corporate and wealthy produced widespread disaster.

There is literally not one single example of any country in the world that put into place neoliberal policies that hasn't turned into a violent police state (Chile), devastated its own working class while producing a bumper crop of billionaires (in the United States and the United Kingdom), or both (Russia).

CHAPTER 6

Milton Friedman Hearts General Pinochet

One of the most famous examples of neoliberal shock to a nation's system came in Chile half a century ago.

In 1971, Chile accounted for 20 percent of the world's known copper reserves; copper was then the world's most valuable commercial metal (iron was number two) and represented fully three-quarters of that nation's export earnings.[1] And those earnings represented only a small portion of the actual value of the copper that Chile exported, because three massive American companies, Anaconda, Kennecott, and Cerro (referred to by Chileans as the Gran Minería), claimed to own roughly 80 percent of all that nation's copper, remnants of 19th-century US claims to the mines.

The Chilean people had long chafed under this foreign ownership and exploitation of the nation's single largest asset, as well as the way these foreign companies treated Chilean workers and miners.

Under President Eduardo Frei Montalva, through the 1960s the country negotiated a gradual and partial purchase of about half of the mines from the companies, but there was still widespread popular discontent around the issue.[2] Imagine how Texans might feel, for example, if 80 percent of all the oil and natural gas in that state were owned by Mexican companies and shipped to Mexico without any reimbursement other than paying taxes to the state of Texas.

As a result, Salvador Allende Gossens was elected president in 1970 after campaigning on fully nationalizing what copper was left in the mines (20 percent of the world's reserves). The legislation to do this was presented to the country's parliament in 1971 and overwhelmingly passed, with even the far-right National Party throwing in all their votes.

A Marxist, Allende had already nationalized the country's banks by simply purchasing all the banks' stock on the open market at competitive prices. Over three years he nationalized a total of 91 industries, increasing wages and lifting substantial portions of the working poor out of poverty.

On October 28, 1971, Allende opened a special tribunal in Santiago to determine how much Chile should reimburse the Gran Minería companies. After public hearings, they determined that the companies had done so much damage to both the mines and Chile's working people and economy that the companies should pay Chile for some of the copper they'd recently taken out of the country: Kennecott owed Chile, they said, $310 million; Anaconda owed it $78 million; and Cerro, which had been less exploitative of Chilean workers and resources, would receive $18 million from the Chilean state.[3]

This set off fireworks in Richard Nixon's White House, with Henry Kissinger and Nixon's CIA beside themselves. Nationalization of a country's natural resources was, they believed, the first step down the road toward total communism, even though socialist Allende was a pragmatic politician with no intention of disrupting most of the rest of his country's industries.

Capitalism was generally fine with Allende, so long as businesses were Chilean-owned, paid workers well, and acted responsibly in the nation's interest.

But the pressure was on from the copper giants, and when Allende also took the nation's telecommunications system away from American-owned International Telephone & Telegraph (ITT), which owned 70 percent of the system, Nixon decided to act.

As the *New York Times* reported in July 1973,

> *The International Telephone and Telegraph Corporation submitted to the White House last October an 18-point plan designed to assure that the Government of Chile's Marxist president, Salvador Allende Gossens, "does not get through the crucial next six months." . . .*
>
> *The I.T.T. plan called for extensive economic warfare against Chile to be directed by a special White House task force, assisted by the Central Intelligence Agency; the subversion of the Chilean armed forces; consultations with foreign governments on ways to put pressure on the Allende regime, and diplomatic sabotage.*[4]

Nixon authorized $10 million for a covert operation in Chile, specifying that the US Embassy in Santiago was to know nothing about it.[5]

Allende was tremendously popular in Chile. While Richard Nixon had been elected president in 1972 with the votes of only 35 percent of eligible American voters, Allende's party had won 37 percent of the 1970 popular vote. He was then elected president by an overwhelming majority in the Parliament, and 800,000 people—one-tenth of the entire population of Chile—showed up in Santiago for a huge celebration.

Nixon, Kissinger, and the CIA decided to take action and launched a campaign against Allende that included economic pressure and an alignment with the Chilean military through a general who'd led the so-called Nazi Cell within the Chilean army, firing on and killing striking workers in 1967. General Augusto Pinochet had "been several times to the U.S. Southern Command schools in the Panama Canal Zone and had served as military attaché in Washington," having famously said, "The army's duty is to kill."[6]

On September 11, 1973—a 9/11 that Chileans claim as their own—General Pinochet rolled his tanks and led his soldiers into Santiago while the army and air force bombed the presidential palace. The attack was preceded by hundreds of truckers (some funded and guided by ITT and the CIA) blocking parts of the city for weeks, shutting down commerce to protest the left-wing tilt of the Allende government.[7]

President Allende gave a final address to the nation via radio; then, seeing where things were heading, he shot himself in the head.

The violent coup was a shock to Chile. The country had one of the most advanced democracies on the continent, having had 160 years of elected governments, the most recent run of democracy in the country lasting 41 years until Pinochet and the CIA took it down.

But Pinochet and the CIA had done their homework; the entire Chilean military went along with the coup. They proceeded to round up the opposition, arresting and imprisoning over 13,000 people who were seen as allies and supporters of the Allende government. Thousands were taken to the National Stadium, where many were tortured and hundreds were executed. As Rupert Cornwall noted in *The Independent*, those numbers didn't even include the "200,000 people who were forced into exile to escape persecution or worse."[8]

By way of intimidating any Chileans who might think about joining opposition to Pinochet's government, the military routinely left mutilated bodies on roadsides and in the country's drainage and irrigation canals.

As Jonathan Kandell wrote in the *New York Times* when Pinochet died:

> [D]uring his rule, more than 3,200 people were executed or disappeared, and scores of thousands more were detained and tortured or exiled....
>
> The press was censored, and labor strikes and unions were banned. A fearsome security apparatus known as the National Intelligence Directorate, or DINA, persecuted, tortured and killed Pinochet opponents within Chile and sometimes beyond its borders. A government-commissioned report issued in 2004 concluded that almost 28,000 people had been tortured during the general's rule....
>
> Tens of thousands of Allende sympathizers were rounded up and brutally interrogated. A majority of the killings took place in the first three months, long after resistance had ended. In most cases, prisoners from a slum or agrarian community would be executed as a means of terrorizing their neighbors into accepting military rule. The killings were often cynically, and falsely, justified as cases in which prisoners were shot while trying to escape.[9]

The blank slate of a new Chile offered the perfect laboratory for Milton Friedman's Chicago Boys to try out their exciting new neoliberal experiment. With encouragement from Nixon's administration, Pinochet brought in a group of economists who'd studied under Friedman and his acolytes, including Chilean economist Sergio de Castro.

They privatized most of the industries Allende had nationalized, threw open the nation's retail systems to foreign-made products, abandoned wage and price regulations and labor protections, and increased military spending while cutting overall government spending by 10 percent. Pinochet even privatized the nation's social security system, turning it over to the newly privatized banks.

The result was an official 375 percent rate of inflation in 1974 (the highest in the world at that time) as cheap imports flooded the country, factories shut down, and workers and families were thrown onto the streets. Food and other necessities were estimated to have gone up as much as 1,000 percent in price as malnutrition and hunger haunted the nation's children.[10]

The Chicago Boys were in a crisis, as their experiment seemed to be collapsing all around them, so they persuaded Pinochet to bring Milton Friedman himself to Chile to encourage people to continue with the Grand Experiment.

In Friedman's memoir coauthored with his wife, *Two Lucky People*, he described what he laid out to the Chilean people during his March 1975 visit. "If this shock approach were adopted," he wrote, "I believe it should be announced publicly in great detail, to take effect at a very close date."[11]

Pinochet's 10 percent cut in government spending was way too timid, Friedman thought. Instead, he wrote, it should include "[a] commitment by the government to reduce government spending by 25 percent within six months, the reduction to take the form of across-the-board reduction of every separate budget by 25 percent, the personnel separations [firings of government employees] to take place as soon as possible."

This gutting of the Chilean government wouldn't really have much impact on the average person, Friedman said. "The discharge of present government employees will not reduce output but simply eliminate waste—their discharge will not mean the production of one fewer pair of shoes or one fewer loaf of bread."

Betraying a certain self-consciousness, he added, "[S]ome of the poorest classes will be affected and whether they are or not, the program will be blamed for their distress."

Summarizing his message to Pinochet and the Chilean people, Friedman wrote, "Such a shock program could end inflation in months and would set the stage for the solution of your second major problem—promoting an effective social market economy."

The problems with Chile's economy two years into the Chicago Boys' and Pinochet's grand experiment were not at all the fault of Friedman's neoliberal prescription, he wrote. "This problem is not of recent origin. It arises from trends toward socialism that started forty years ago and reached their logical—and terrible—climax in the Allende regime. You have been extremely wise in adopting the many measures you have already taken to reverse this trend."

Pinochet took Friedman's advice to heart, and by 1980, public spending under Pinochet was half what it had been when he seized power. But the economy was still in crisis.

"Undeterred," Naomi Klein wrote in *Shock Doctrine*, "Pinochet's economic team went into more experimental territory, introducing Friedman's most vanguard policies: the public school system was replaced by vouchers and charter schools, health care became pay-as-you-go, and kindergartens and cemeteries were privatized. Most radical of all, they privatized Chile's social security system."

Ironically, Klein noted, "[t]he only thing that protected Chile from complete economic collapse in the early eighties was that Pinochet had never privatized Codelco, the state copper mine company nationalized by Allende. That one company generated 85 percent of Chile's export revenues, which meant that when the financial bubble burst, the state still had a steady source of funds."[12]

In the end, it had all been a futile exercise, as the *New York Times* said in Pinochet's December 11, 2006, obituary: "But by the time of his death, even some of those economic victories had been called into question. The privatizing of Chile's social security system, in particular, has come under attack as unjust and is undergoing revision. And across Latin America, many of the countries that had adopted similar reforms are reversing some of them, responding to a growing wave of popular, leftist anger over untrammeled foreign competition and unequal distribution of wealth."[13]

The neoliberals still largely control Chile, although they've become more like Bill Clinton than Augusto Pinochet. But the results are visible. Chile has Latin America's top gross domestic product (GDP) per capita, but that income and wealth is hardly well distributed; its poverty level is even higher than that of Brazil.

As economics scholar Branko Milanovic wrote in November 2019, "The bottom 5 percent of Chile's population have an income level that is about the same as that of the bottom 5 percent in Mongolia. The top 2 percent enjoy an income level equivalent to that of the top 2 percent in Germany.... Chile is the country where billionaires' share, in terms of GDP, is the highest in the world.... The wealth of Chile's billionaires, compared to their country's GDP, exceeds even that of Russia's."[14]

In his book *The Pinochet File*, Peter Kornbluh reported, "The military regime's problems began in mid-1982 when the country suffered its worst economic recession since the Great Depression. Gross national product plummeted by 14 percent; unemployment rose to 30 percent. Chile's foreign debt reached $19 billion, then the highest per-capita debt in the world. The 'economic miracle' created by the University of Chicago–trained students of free-market guru and regime adviser Milton Friedman was discredited."[15]

Although neoliberal "scholars" and think tanks funded by American right-wing billionaires have gone to astonishing lengths to try to portray Friedman and Pinochet's experiment with neoliberalism a success (just check the internet: there are 20 praising them for every one criticizing them), the simple reality is that the Chilean experiment, the world's first real try at neoliberalism, failed utterly ... and killed a lot of people in the process.

CHAPTER 7

Neoliberalism Comes to America

In America, it was inflation that opened the door to Milton Friedman's neoliberalism.

Inflation is usually caused by one of two things: international devaluation or internal dilution of a country's currency, or widespread shortages of essential commodities that drive up prices enough to echo through the entire economy.

The early 1970s got both, one deliberately and the other as the result of war.

Between 1971 and 1973, President Nixon pulled the United States out of the Bretton Woods economic framework that had been put together after World War II to stabilize the world's currencies and balance trade. The dollar had been pegged to gold at $35 an ounce, and the world's other currencies were effectively pegged to the dollar.

But the United States couldn't buy enough gold to support the number of dollars we needed as our economy grew, so on August 15, 1971, Nixon announced to the nation and the world that he was taking the dollar off the gold standard and putting a 10 percent tariff on most imports of finished goods into the US to deal with the changes in the dollar's value relative to other currencies.

The immediate result was that the value of the dollar rose as the world breathed a sigh of relief that the "gold crisis" was coming to an end and the dollar would become more portable. But an increased value in the dollar relative to other currencies meant that products manufactured in the US became more expensive overseas, hurting our exports.

At that time, there were 60,000 more factories in the US than today, and Walmart was advertising that everything in their stores was "Made in the USA":[1] exports were an important part of our economy, and imports were mostly raw materials or "exotic" goods not produced here, like sandalwood from Thailand or French wines.[2]

To deal with the "strong dollar" problem, Nixon announced in December 1971 that the US was devaluing our currency relative to the Japanese yen, German mark, and British pound (among others) by 11 percent. It was the first-ever negotiated realignment of the world's major currencies, and Nixon crowed that it was "the greatest monetary agreement in the history of the world."

But we were still importing more and more goods from overseas, particularly cars from Japan, increasing our trade deficit and hurting American jobs that manufactured goods like cars that competed with the Japanese and the Germans. So in the second week of February 1973, Nixon did it again, negotiating a further devaluation of the dollar by 10 percent.[3]

While devaluing the dollar against other currencies didn't have much immediate impact on products grown or made in the United States from US raw materials, it did mean that the prices of imports (including oil, which was the primary energy supply for pretty much everything in America) went up.

Over the next decade, the impact of that devaluation would work its way through the American economy in the form of a mild inflation, which Nixon thought could be easily controlled by Fed monetary policy.

What he hadn't figured on, though, was the 1973 Arab-Israeli War. Because America took Israel's side in the war, the Arab states cut off their supply of oil to the US in October 1973. As the State Department's history of the time notes, "The price of oil per barrel first doubled, then quadrupled, imposing skyrocketing costs on consumers and structural challenges to the stability of whole national economies."[4]

Everything in America depended on oil, from manufacturing fertilizer to powering tractors, from lighting up cities to moving cars and trucks down the highway, from heating homes to powering factories. As a result, the price of everything went up: it was a classic supply-shock-driven inflation.

The war ended on January 19, 1974, and the Arab nations lifted their embargo on oil to the US in March of that year.[5] Between two devaluations and the explosion in oil prices, inflation in the US was running red-hot by the mid-1970s, and it would take about a decade for it to be wrung out of our economy through Fed actions and normal readjustments in the international and domestic marketplace.

But Americans were furious. The price of pretty much everything was up by 10 percent or more, and wages weren't keeping pace. Strikes started to roil the economy as Nixon was busted for accepting bribes and authorizing a break-in at the Democratic National Committee's headquarters in the Watergate complex. Nixon left office and Gerald Ford became our president, launching his campaign to stabilize the dollar with a nationally televised speech on October 8, 1974.[6]

Ford's program included a temporary 5 percent increase in top-end income taxes, cuts to federal spending, and "the creation of a voluntary inflation-fighting organization, named 'Whip Inflation Now' (WIN)."[7] The inflation rate in 1974 peaked at 12.3 percent, and home mortgage rates were going through the roof.

WIN became a joke, inflation persisted and got worse as we became locked into a wage-price spiral (particularly after Nixon's wage-price controls ended), and President Ford was replaced by President Jimmy Carter in the election of 1976.

But inflation persisted as the realignment of the US dollar and the price of oil was forcing a market response to the value of the dollar. (An x percent annual inflation rate means, practically speaking, that the dollar has lost x percent of its value that year.)

The inflation rates for 1977, 1978, 1979, and 1980 were, respectively, 6.7 percent, 9.0 percent, 13.3 percent, and 12.5 percent.[8]

In 1978, Margaret Thatcher came to power in the United Kingdom and, advised by neoliberals at the Institute of Economic Affairs (IEA), a UK-based private think tank, began a massive program of crushing that country's labor unions while privatizing as much of the country's infrastructure as she could, up to and including British Airways and British Rail.

She appointed Geoffrey Howe, a member of the Mont Pelerin Society and friend of Milton Friedman's, as her chancellor of the exchequer (like the American secretary of the Treasury) to run the British economy. Friedman, crowing about his own influence on Howe and the IEA's founder, Sir Antony Fisher, wrote, "The U-turn in British policy executed by Margaret Thatcher owes more to him (i.e., Fisher) than any other individual."[9]

The ideas of neoliberalism had, by this time, spread across the world, and Thatcher's UK was getting international applause for being the world's first major economy to put them into place. Pressure built on President Carter to do the same, and, hoping it might help whip inflation, he deregulated the US trucking and airline industries, among others, in the last two years of his presidency.

Ronald Reagan was elected in 1980, and when he came into office, he jumped into neoliberal policy with both feet, starting by crushing the air traffic controllers' union, PATCO, in a single week. Union busting, welfare cutting, free trade, and deregulation were the themes of Reagan's eight years, then carried on another four years by President George H. W. Bush, whose administration negotiated the North American Free Trade Agreement (NAFTA).

America was now officially on the neoliberal path, and Friedman and his Mont Pelerin buddies were cheering it on.

By 1982, inflation was down from 1981's 8.9 percent to a respectable and tolerable 3.8 percent; it averaged around that for the rest of the decade. Instead of pointing out that it normally takes a supply-shock inflation and a currency-devaluation inflation a decade or two to work itself out, the American media gave Reagan and neoliberalism all the credit.[10] Milton Friedman, after all, had made his reputation as the great scholar of inflation and was a relentless self-promoter, appearing in newspapers and newsmagazines almost every week in one way or another.

Claiming that neoliberal policies had crushed over a decade of inflation in a single year, and ignoring the fact that it was just the normal wringing-out of inflation from the economy, Reagan openly embraced neoliberalism with a passion at every level of his administration. He embarked on a series of massive tax cuts for the morbidly rich, dropping the top tax bracket from 74 percent when he came into office down to 25 percent. He borrowed the money to pay for it, tripling the national debt from roughly $800 billion in 1980 to $2.4 trillion when he left office, and the effect of that $2 trillion he put on the nation's credit card was a sharp economic stimulus for which Reagan took the credit.

He deregulated financial markets and savings and loan (S&L) banks, letting Wall Street raiders walk away with billions while gutting S&Ls so badly that the federal government had to bail out the industry by replacing about $100 billion that the bankers had stolen.[11]

"Greed is good!" was the new slogan, junk bonds became a thing, and mergers and acquisitions experts, or "M&A Artists" who called themselves "Masters of the Universe," became the nation's heroes, lionized in movies like the 1987 *Wall Street*, starring Michael Douglas.

Reagan signed Executive Order 12291, which required all federal agencies to use a cost-benefit estimate when putting together federal rules and regulations. Instead of considering costs of externalities (things like the damage that pollution does to people or how bank rip-offs hurt the middle class), however, the only costs his administration worried about were expenses to industry.

He cut the regulatory power of the Environmental Protection Agency (EPA), and his head of that organization, Anne Gorsuch (mother of Supreme Court Justice Neil Gorsuch), was, as *Newsweek* reported, "involved in a nasty scandal involving political manipulation, fund mismanagement, perjury and destruction of subpoenaed documents," leaving office in disgrace.[12]

Meanwhile, Reagan's secretary of the interior, James Watt, went on a binge selling off federal lands to drilling and mining interests for pennies on the dollar. When asked if he was concerned about the environmental destruction of sensitive lands, he replied, "[M]y responsibility is to follow the Scriptures which call upon us to occupy the land until Jesus returns."[13] According to Watt's fundamentalist dogma, any damage to the environment would be reversed when Jesus came back to Earth and would "[make] all things new."

Reagan cut education funding, putting Bill Bennett in as secretary of education. Bennett was a big advocate of the so-called school choice movement that emerged in the wake of the 1954 Supreme Court *Brown v. Board of Education* decision, which ordered school desegregation. All-white private, religious, and charter schools started getting federal dollars; public schools had their funds cut; and Bennett later rationalized it all by saying, "If it were your sole purpose to reduce crime, you could abort every black baby in this country, and your crime rate would go down."[14]

The Labor Department had been created back in 1913 by President William H. Taft, a progressive Republican,[15] and

Reagan installed former construction executive Ray Donovan as its head, the first anti-labor partisan to ever run the department, a position he had to leave when he was indicted for fraud and grand larceny (the charges didn't stick) related to Mafia associates he was in tight with. As the *Washington Post* observed when Donovan died, "Carrying out Reagan's conservative agenda, Mr. Donovan eased regulations for business, including Occupational Safety and Health Administration rules disliked by industry. He withdrew a rule requiring the labeling of hazardous chemicals in the workplace and postponed federal employment and training programs, equal opportunity employment measures, and a minimum-wage increase for service workers. His tenure also saw drastic cuts in the department's budget and staff."[16]

That sort of thing happened in every federal agency throughout the Reagan and Bush presidencies; much of their neoliberal damage has yet to be undone.

By 1992, Americans were starting to wise up to Reagan's scam.

Thousands of factories had closed, their production shipped overseas; working-class wages had stagnated since his first year in office, while CEO salaries exploded from 29 times the average worker's salary in 1978 to 129 times average worker wages in 1995 (they're over 300 times average worker wages today);[17] and union membership had dropped from a third of workers to around 15 percent (it's around 6 percent of the private workforce today).[18]

The Reagan and Bush administrations negotiated the neo-liberal centerpiece, the NAFTA treaty (although they called it a "trade agreement" rather than a treaty because it couldn't get past the constitutional requirement for a two-thirds vote in the Senate to approve all treaties), and wanted it signed the following year, in 1993.

CHAPTER 8

Bill Clinton Hearts the Neoliberal Revolution

Texas billionaire Ross Perot jumped into the 1992 presidential race to take on the two neoliberal "free traders" George H. W. Bush and Bill Clinton. If America signed NAFTA, Perot warned, there would be "a giant sucking sound" from the south pulling jobs out of America.[1]

Worse, Perot warned, this would eventually become a national security issue: when we reached the point where we couldn't make an aircraft carrier or missile without parts from China or another foreign country, our ability to defend ourselves would be severely compromised.

"If we keep shifting our manufacturing jobs across the border and around the world and deindustrializing our country," Perot said, "we will not be able to defend this great country."[2] And today, as CBS News reports, we're there: "The hellfire missile—launched from helicopters, jets and predator drones—has been a critical weapon in the war on terror. But the propellant that fires the missile must be imported from China."[3]

The 1992 election represented the first American revolt against neoliberalism: Perot took almost 20 percent of all votes. Bill Clinton was elected with only a 43 percent plurality of the vote.

Perot's movement aside, by 1993 the Democratic Party had largely embraced a slightly softer (still allowing for public schools and some social programs) form of neoliberalism.

The American and British groupthink consensus across major political parties was that Freidman and his Mont Pelerin buddies were right: the rich should rule the world, labor unions were a pain in the ass, and government regulation simply stifled innovation.

Everything that could be privatized should be, and stockholder returns should be the only metric that business used for decision-making, discarding old notions of corporate responsibility to workers, customers, communities, and even the institution of the corporation itself. If increasing profits and thus dividends meant screwing workers, producing substandard products, demanding huge tax breaks from or polluting communities, or even breaking up and selling off the company, so be it. Even the Supreme Court was now onboard, having fully embraced Robert Bork's notion that profits were the singular North Star.[4]

Reagan's destruction of the union movement added a critical problem for the Democrats: unions had been their major funding source. Democratic consultant Al From came up with the idea of the party embracing corporate America and neoliberal ideology to make up for the lost union money; he traveled to Arkansas to pitch it to Governor Bill Clinton, who agreed to run for president on that platform.

From later (2013) wrote a book about the experience and the need for the party to run and govern on the basis of "economic centrism, national security, and entitlement reform."[5]

Democrats had now joined Republicans in the back pocket of American business, although to differentiate themselves they embraced "clean" industries like banking, insurance, and tech, leaving money from the "dirty" industries like coal, oil, and chemicals to the Republicans.

Clinton embraced with gusto the neoliberal idea that free trade was the ultimate way to end wars between nations. In December 1996, *New York Times* columnist Thomas Friedman (no relation to Milton) laid out what came to be called the McDonald's Doctrine, positing that no two nations that each had a McDonald's would ever go to war.[6] (In a more recent column, he revised the idea from the Golden Arches Theory of Conflict Prevention to the Dell Theory of Conflict Prevention.)

After all, when nations are economically interconnected, don't they have an incentive to not bust up that relationship with something as gross as military conflict?

The idea was an idiocy on its face then and still is today, but it flew. Books were published, articles written, speeches given. Free trade agreements flowed like champagne while America continued to hemorrhage good-paying manufacturing jobs and slid toward becoming a "Do you want fries with that?" service economy.

Clinton also took a meat-ax to the nation's welfare programs, apparently convinced of the conservative message that even survival-level benefits caused laziness—or he'd decided that buying into that myth was politically useful.

If that premise were true, by the way, it would be a great selling point for taxing all inheritances at 100 percent. After all, who would want to inflict laziness on their children by leaving them enough money that they didn't need to work?

But, of course, it was just another idiocy promoted by the very rich (who pass along their wealth to their children without worrying that it'll cause laziness) to justify cutting tax-funded programs for "lower class" folks, particularly people of color, so they could keep their tax dollars in their money bins.

Nonetheless, Clinton proudly declared in a State of the Union speech that he had brought about "the end of welfare as we know it."

Meanwhile, the Soviet Union had undergone a controlled demolition, guided by the hand of Mikhail Gorbachev, who genuinely hoped to turn his nation from a corrupt communist oligarchy into a democratic-socialist success story along the lines of the Scandinavian countries.

Gorby explicitly hoped for Russia to emulate Sweden and become a "socialist beacon for the world," as described by Lawrence Klein and Marshall Pomer in their book *The New Russia: Transition Gone Awry.*[7]

In December 2015, Louise and I attended a banquet in Moscow with former President Gorbachev, President Vladimir Putin, and a few dozen others. Gorbachev, who had spent hours with my friend and colleague Leila Conners (we made several environmental documentaries together, along with Leonardo DiCaprio) for her movie *The Arrow of Time*, still hoped for the best.

"Many of these ideas might appear utopian or unachievable in the context of the present political order," he'd told Leila a few years earlier when the movie premiered in Switzerland,

"and that is precisely because they address the roots of the current issues."

Nonetheless, when I saw Gorbachev in 2015, he looked like a broken man. His project to create a Scandinavian-style democracy had been hijacked by George H. W. Bush and other leaders of the G7 countries at a meeting of that group in 1991 when they explicitly told him that he must embrace neoliberalism if he wanted Western loans to help with his transition project.

"Their suggestions as to the tempo and methods of transition," Gorbachev is quoted in *The New Russia*, "were astonishing."

In *The Shock Doctrine*, Naomi Klein quoted the Russian newspaper *Nezavisimaya Gazeta*'s observation at that time that "for the first time Russia will get in its government a team of [neo]liberals who consider themselves followers of Friedrich von Hayek and the 'Chicago school' of Milton Friedman."[8]

Klein then chronicled the outcome after a single year of Friedman's reforms:

After only one year, shock therapy had taken a devastating toll: millions of middle-class Russians had lost their life savings when money lost its value, and abrupt cuts to subsidies meant millions of workers had not been paid in months. The average Russian consumed 40 percent less in 1992 than 1991, and a third of the population fell below the poverty line. The middle class was forced to sell personal belongings from card tables on the streets—desperate acts that the Chicago School economists praised as "entrepreneurial," proof that a capitalist renaissance was indeed

under way, one family heirloom and second-hand blazer at
a time.

The country was gutted like a fish, its assets sold off for pennies on the dollar to the men who we now know as "Russian oligarchs," fabulously rich billionaires who float above the Russian landscape the way Jeff Bezos blasts himself into outer space over America.

In December 1994, I was working with the German-based international relief organization Salem International and visited their newest project in Kaliningrad, Russia. It brought me face-to-face with the destruction of the Chicago Boys' neoliberal reforms: vodka was cheaper than potable water, organized crime ran most of the commerce in the city, and the families I visited kept baskets filled with scraps of newspaper next to their toilets to use as toilet paper.

This city, where Immanuel Kant once lived, had disintegrated after its parts had been stripped, monetized, and sold off to the highest bidders. Here's an excerpt from the diary I kept of that trip:

I landed at about noon on a gray, blustery, raw-cold day in
Kaliningrad. . . . A once-beautiful old river, now black and
fouled with sewage and industrial waste, runs through the
city. . . .

Herr Burkhardt took me for an afternoon walk. A cold
wind cut through the stone streets, and most of the buildings
looked like a typical 19th-century (or earlier) European
city, although there was no color anywhere. No paint, no
signs, no colorful curtains. Everything was gray, from the

leaden sky to the grime-covered buildings to the slushy sidewalks and cobblestone streets.

We crossed the river on a long bridge and walked a few
blocks into town, navigating around gaping 2-foot-diameter
open manholes in the middle of the sidewalks, opening down
into black pools of sewage ten feet below the surface.

The streets were filled with people, bundled against the
wind, their faces lined and cracked by weather and hard
lives in this dismal place. I saw not a single smile: everybody
seemed in a hurry to get somewhere, and few people talked
among themselves. . . .

Back at Olga's house, the TV was on in the living room.
. . . When the show ended, a man's face filled the screen. He
was giving some sort of speech, and his face was twisted with
an insane anger. He pounded his fist and shook his finger at
the camera, then became soft and soothing in his voice, then
began shouting again. He was followed by what was obvi-
ously a news anchorwoman, sitting behind a desk, making
commentary.

"What's that?" I said to the room in general.

"Vladimir Zhirinovsky [the extreme right-wing candi-
date]," said Olga in German. "He's a candidate for president, and he said that if he's elected, then we should work
more closely with Germany, reestablish our old border with
them."

"Isn't Poland in between you and Germany?"

"That's what he means," Olga said, shaking her head in
disbelief. "Get rid of Poland."

I shivered.

Boris Yeltsin won reelection in 1996 and continued his neo-liberal reforms with the help of the Chicago Boys, paving the way for Vladimir Putin's rise to the presidency in 2000, finally killing altogether Gorbachev's Scandinavian hopes. Russia is truly the clearest example of the consequences of full-blown neoliberalism, and Zhirinovsky was their version of Donald Trump, who himself rose to power in America as a backlash against 40 years of somewhat slower and softer neoliberalism here.

Back in America, the zeitgeist of the era was personified by the hot new thing for Democrats to do in the Clinton '90s: make an annual pilgrimage to the World Economic Forum at Davos, Switzerland, to rub elbows with the world's bankers and billionaires. Philanthropy could take care of people's needs, the neoliberal billionaires asserted, and in his 1996 State of the Union speech, Clinton declared, "The era of big government is over."[9]

Taking that theory to its logical next step, in 1999 Clinton signed the Financial Services Modernization Act (FSMA), which unraveled banking regulations dating back to FDR's Glass-Steagall Act, which outlawed the dangerous 1920s practice of banks gambling in the stock or other markets with depositors' money.[10]

CHAPTER 9

George W. Bush Pushes Neoliberalism Even Further

By the time George W. Bush became president in January 2001, neoliberalism had defeated even the Perot faction of American thought: politicians who opposed it, like Bernie Sanders and Sherrod Brown on the left and Mike Lee and Ron Paul on the right, were dismissed as cranks and outliers trying to stand in the way of progress.

Bush continued the process, with his largest success being the privatization, with the Medicare Modernization Act of 2003, of a large chunk of the nation's premier government-funded health care program, Medicare.

The new Medicare Advantage programs, entirely run by private entities, cost the federal government on average 11 percent more than Medicare and were given the freedom to deny services to their customers the way health insurance companies have been scamming their customers for generations.[1]

I lay this out, chapter and verse, in *The Hidden History of American Healthcare*, but suffice it to say that by this writing, nearly half of the entire Medicare program has now been replaced by fully privatized health insurance under the deceptive rubric of Medicare Advantage, while Medicare itself has been seriously defunded by the transfer of so many billions to the bottom lines of Advantage providers.

Bush also used the excuse of the deregulation of the banking industry in 1999 to look the other way as his morbidly rich donors in the financial services industry created hundreds of exotic new "products" to sell to investors, the most notorious being collateralized debt obligations (CDOs) used to bundle fraudulent home mortgages in with good ones to disguise their provenance and risks.

Bankers like California's notorious "Foreclosure King" Steven Mnuchin became fabulously rich, picking up a private jet and multimillion-dollar mansion while the nation's economy inched further and further out onto thin ice.[2]

Through it all, despite a few warning voices, the Bush administration and the neoliberal-leaning governments of Europe's largest nations all reassured us that the market operated on its own "magic invisible hand" rules and there was nothing to worry about. Just trust the market and the market-makers. They know what they're doing.

And, indeed, they did know what they were doing. Just like John Dillinger and Ken Lay did. They extracted literally trillions of dollars out of the United States and other Western economies and then stood back, feigning helplessness, when it all collapsed in the "Bush Crash" of 2008.

In response to the crisis that bankers had created, governments around the world shoveled money at those very same bankers and their institutions. "The total potential federal government support could reach up to $23.7 trillion" is what Neil Barofsky, special inspector general for the Troubled Asset Relief Program (TARP), reported to Congress in 2008.[3]

While the actual American part of the banker bailout was probably closer to $5 trillion, by 2010 the bankers were giving each other billion-dollar bonuses and diving off the high boards into their money bins.

It's almost as if Milton Friedman had planned it; after all, his first step out of academia and into paid shilling for industry and the ultrarich was to author that notorious 1946 pamphlet for the real estate industry advocating total deregulation of both the real estate business and the banks that offered mortgages.

Bush's other big neoliberal experiment was with the government of Iraq. His brother Jeb Bush, along with his defense secretary, Donald Rumsfeld; his vice president, Dick Cheney; and his advisers Paul Wolfowitz, Bill Kristol, and John Bolton had all signed on to the notorious 1998 Project for a New American Century statement calling on then-President Bill Clinton to immediately invade Iraq and expel Saddam Hussein.[4]

As Cheney would later state, Iraq was sitting atop the second-largest single-country reserve of oil in the world, just behind Saudi Arabia. "He sits on top of 10 per cent of the world's oil reserves," Cheney said, adding, "He has enormous wealth being generated by that."[5]

While former Halliburton Company chief Cheney was salivating over the prospect of seizing and selling all that oil, George W. Bush saw a war in Iraq as a way to guarantee his own reelection in 2004.

Back in 1999, writer Mickey Herskowitz, hired by the Bush family to ghostwrite Bush's autobiography *A Charge to Keep*,[6] explained that Bush told him, "One of the keys to being seen as a great leader is to be seen as a commander-in-chief. . . . My father had all this political capital built up when he drove the Iraqis out of Kuwait and he wasted it. . . . If I have a chance to invade, if I had that much capital, I'm not going to waste it. I'm going to get everything passed that I want to get passed and I'm going to have a successful presidency."[7]

Bush wasn't much of an ideologue, and it's unlikely that he could have even explained neoliberalism, but his defense secretary, Donald Rumsfeld, was both a student and a close personal friend of Milton Friedman's and an ardent neoliberal.

Once Iraq was conquered and Saddam Hussein was dead, Rumsfeld put former Kissinger Associates managing director L. Paul Bremer III in charge of the country. Bremer, the wealthy son of the former CEO of Christian Dior, had been educated in the world's best private schools, from Phillips Academy Andover to Yale University to the Paris Institute of Political Studies. He knew the rich and powerful of the world—he was one of them—and had been Rumsfeld's assistant in the first Bush administration overseeing the first Gulf War against Saddam.

Bremer followed the Mont Pelerin neoliberal script to the last detail. The Iraqi army was the nation's largest employer, with over half a million men drawing a weekly paycheck and each having an AK-47 handy in their homes. Bremer fired them all, creating an instant and well-armed insurgency of pissed-off formerly middle-class soldiers.

He also shut down almost all of the hundreds of government-owned companies, manufacturing steel to machine tools to cement and military goods.

Bremer threw open the country to the world's predatory corporations, eliminating *all* tariffs and trade regulations, while standing aside as the nation's government-run libraries and museums were looted on behalf of wealthy foreign antiquities collectors. All of this was a clear violation of international law that prevents winners in wars from looting the countries they've conquered, but neoliberals around the world had always ignored such laws.

Rumsfeld defended the video of looters carrying off 3,000-year-old irreplaceable artifacts with the glib "Freedom's untidy, and free people are free to make mistakes and commit crimes and do bad things." When asked if looting was the inevitable consequence of Rumsfeld's "freedom," he replied, as CNN reported, "Stuff happens."[8]

Bremer then threw out Iraq's progressive corporate and individual income taxes, which peaked at 45 percent, and replaced them with Milton Friedman's beloved 15 percent flat tax, a huge windfall for Iraq's wealthy elite but a massive and sudden tax increase for the country's low-income workers.

He ended Iraq's laws requiring domestic ownership of major industries, allowing foreigners to buy and own 100 percent of pretty much anything—from land to oil to businesses—and take up to 100 percent of their profits out of the country tax-free.[9]

After neoliberalism had failed spectacularly in Chile, gutted the American and British middle classes, and flipped Russia from a brief democracy into a brutal oligarchy, Iraq was to be the final proof that it could work.

Wolfowitz, Bremer, and neoliberal apologists around the world promised that the country would soon flower, as the free market, lacking government regulation and with minimal taxation, would solve all problems, from poverty to political corruption to meeting the people's basic food, housing, and safety needs.

It didn't work out that way.

Instead of a million flowers blossoming in the soil of neoliberal freedom, over 1.2 million Iraqis lost their homes and became internal refugees,[10] nearly half a million fled the country (those with the wealth to get out), and 288,000 died as a direct consequence of the American invasion.[11]

And that doesn't begin to account for generations of trauma and PTSD, destroyed infrastructure and torn-apart families, and the shattering of America's image and influence around the world.

Twenty years later, with the neoliberal project largely abandoned and *never* mentioned out loud by its champions, Iraq is still staggering, plagued by political instability, disease, and an Iraqi warlord version of the oligarchic political culture that neoliberalism always produces.

Neoliberalism Blows Up in Bush's Face

Meanwhile, back in America, neoliberal policies brought our government and economic system to its knees in the last year of Bush's presidency. Banks, investment houses, and real estate speculators had been deregulated nine years earlier and used their new freedom to essentially rob, rape, and pillage the American financial landscape.

In the process, corrupt financial operations and betting on stocks became a huge part of the American economy.

The greatest damage to America came because loaning, borrowing, and trading money and securities produces absolutely nothing of lasting value to a country. It's not at all like manufacturing, where applying labor to raw materials produces products that have lasting value.

Instead, unregulated finance extracts massive amounts of cash as commissions and fees for a small number of fabulously wealthy and powerful Wall Street giants, reducing resources that could instead be used to manufacture things that do add value for generations.

But don't just take my word for it. Jack Bogle was the guy who created the first widely traded index fund, the Vanguard 500, back in 1976. Although he stepped down as chairman of the company in 1999, he opined long after about the state of the economy and, in a moment of extraordinary candor, told reporters for *Money* magazine in 2015, "The job of finance is to provide capital to companies. We do it to the tune of $250 billion a year in IPOs and secondary offerings. What else do we do? We encourage investors to trade about $32 trillion a year. So the way I calculate it, 99% of what we do in this industry is people trading with one another, with a gain only to the middleman. It's a waste of resources."[1]

In 2008, the bill came due for the trillions of dollars that speculators, hedge funds, mortgage bankers, and other predators in the financial services industry had extracted from the American and world economies.

It started in 2000, after the 1999 neoliberal deregulation of America's banks: bankers went on a lending spree to would-be homeowners, offering them mortgages with no income or asset requirements (sometimes called *liar loans*).

Because this practice was injecting so much new money into the housing market, housing prices soared; many of the no-asset home purchasers were average people trying to be real estate speculators, figuring they'd buy a house, hold it for a year or two, and sell it for a solid profit.

House flipping became a thing.

All across America, telephone poles had flyers on them for "real estate seminars" promising to teach average folks how to make money in the housing market just like the billionaire bankers did. It was a national celebration of get-rich-quick grifting.

One of the larger grifts in this marketplace, for example, was Trump University. As the *Washington Post* reported, Trump's sales pitch was "[T]he billionaire had made enough money for himself. Now, he would put his famous brain to work for the little guy."[2]

The liar loans not only let millions of people speculate in the real estate market but also gave an entrée into single-family housing for millions of people whose level of income and assets would have prevented them from borrowing in a regulated market. As long as the economy was good, though, and they had a reliable income, they could hang on to their first homes.

The banks and mortgage houses took those liar loan mortgages, mixed them with "good" assets like mortgages for people with the means to repay their loans, and sold these interest-bearing "products" in the open investment market.

They bribed the credit rating agencies to give them a seal of approval, and banks themselves bought and sold trillions in these collateralized debt obligations and other exotic products.[3]

Because they were generally high-interest loans (because of the borrowers' poor credit ratings), they paid far more than almost any other readily available investments. Throughout the first eight years of the 21st century, they spread into investment portfolios all over the world.

Then came the recession of 2006. The market softened, unemployment went up, and millions were facing foreclosure. Most hung on, driving up credit card or other debt to keep their houses, hoping prices would rise back up enough that they could sell them for what they owed.

That wasn't to happen.

By 2008, the housing market was completely in the tank, and foreclosures had reached the point where the owners of CDOs and other "innovative" investment instruments created out of the 1999 deregulation could no longer ignore the risk of defaults.

January 2008 saw a 57 percent increase in foreclosures over the previous year, and February dropped another 24 percent year-over-year. Resale home prices fell 4.6 percent in January and were down 8.2 percent by the end of February. The system was hemorrhaging cash.[4]

The biggest problem that wealthy and institutional investors in CDOs and other debt instruments had was that, because the market was deregulated and supposedly run by the invisible hand of the marketplace, nobody knew exactly how many bad mortgages were buried in these bundles or what kind of a liability they represented as a share of the United States' $12 trillion mortgage market.[5] Freddie Mac and Fannie Mae alone had taken on $3 trillion in loans all by themselves; the big banks were opaque, and if they knew how much poison they'd packaged, they weren't telling anybody.[6]

Money market funds were heavily invested in these new products and tried to unload them as fast as they could . . . but nobody was buying. Seeing that the funds, which are not federally guaranteed, could fail, investors pulled out cash like there was no tomorrow.

On September 16, the Reserve Primary Fund "broke the buck," meaning they paid back dollars given them with less than a dollar each. The next day, investors pulled a record $172 billion from money market funds, adding to the pressure (normal withdrawals are around $7 billion per day).[7]

By the time of the 2008 election, Congress had poured $700 billion into bailing out bankers, and the Fed had anted up almost $3 trillion, between their $1.7 trillion "commercial loan program," their $540 billion loan to money markets, and their June "Term Auction Facility" loan of $225 billion. The FDIC threw an additional $1.3 trillion into the banking system on November 21.

Wall Street bankers (except for Lehman Brothers, the only bank "allowed to fail") were giving a huge sigh of relief and hurrying to stash their billions of ill-gotten gains in tax havens overseas. At the same time, homeowners across America were being thrown out of their houses in a national tsunami of foreclosures that led to an early explosion in homelessness.

Bankster Steve Mnuchin alone would pick up one of the California banks holding some of this debt and throw 36,000 people out of their homes, each foreclosure earning his company a federal bailout payment and earning him the moniker "The Foreclosure King." This positioned him perfectly for a later job with Donald Trump as the nation's Treasury secretary. His profitable, no-risk strategy was being replicated by banks and mortgage brokers all across the nation.

As fully 10 million Americans lost their homes, Americans began to openly question neoliberalism. On my radio program at the time, I openly speculated that 2008 would go down in history as "the year neoliberalism died in America."

Sadly, I was premature in that proclamation.

CHAPTER 11

Obama Rescues
Neoliberalism from Itself

That year, Barack Obama was elected to the presidency. In his inaugural address in January 2009, he told the American people that markets needed supervision to work.

"Nor is the question before us whether the market is a force for good or ill," President Obama said, looking into the camera. "Its power to generate wealth and expand freedom is unmatched. But this crisis has reminded us that without a watchful eye, the market can spin out of control. The nation cannot prosper long when it favors only the prosperous."

Americans who were hopeful that the age of neoliberalism was coming to an end (even if they didn't know there was a name for it) cheered: Obama's popularity soared above 60 percent.

Instead of ending neoliberalism, though, Obama expanded it dramatically with the Affordable Care Act, putting the nation's health care needs in the hands of billion-dollar insurance companies and extending the privatization of Medicare through the Medicare Advantage scam that George W. Bush had brought into being.

Obama refused to regulate the nation's monopolies, instead extending Bush's Emergency Economic Stabilization Act and TARP, which poured ever-more money into the pockets of Wall Street banksters.

Advised by notorious neoliberal Lawrence Summers (formerly Clinton's Treasury secretary) and former Wall Street banker Timothy Geithner (as Obama's Treasury secretary), Obama passed on the opportunity to reregulate the banks or push for legislation like a revisited Glass-Steagall to prevent checkbook banks from gambling in the stock market with your and my deposits. Instead, he went with the watered-down Dodd-Frank legislation, championed by two noted neoliberal legislators, Sen. Christopher Dodd (D-CT) and Rep. Barney Frank (D-MA), who were both deeply in the pockets of Wall Street banks.[1]

Bankers are still running many of their old scams, even as I write these words in 2022.

Meanwhile, President Obama oversaw without objection the explosion of the neoliberal dream of a so-called gig economy, where companies relabeled their employees as *independent contractors* to avoid insurance, taxes, and the regulations and liabilities that come as an employer.

Even his smallest pushbacks against neoliberalism—including an attempt to raise income taxes on the morbidly rich and advance universal pre-K—were shot down by Republicans and neoconservative Democrats in Congress.

Dissatisfied, Americans decided to try the Republicans again.

CHAPTER 12

Trump Attacks Neoliberalism

One of the key aspects of neoliberalism is the corruption it creates. When trust is placed in the free market instead of government regulators and legal protections, predators and lobbyists have free rein.

Seeing how disgusted Americans were by this fundamental flaw in the neoliberal system, Donald Trump promised to "drain the swamp" of big-money corruption in Washington, DC. He claimed that he knew how the game was played because he had played it himself, buying off politicians whenever necessary.

During the August 2015 GOP primary debate, he called out all the other Republicans on the stage, saying, "I gave [money] to many people, before this; before two months ago, I was a businessman. I give to everybody. When they call, I give. And do you know what? When I need something from them two years later, three years later, I call them, they are there for me."

In September at the next primary debate, he ran that line again, saying, "The donors, the special interests, the lobbyists, have very strong power over these people," as he waved at the other Republicans on the stage. "I am not accepting any money from anybody. Nobody has control of me other than the people of this country."

Trump also campaigned on ending neoliberal free trade policy and even threw a bone in that direction after he became president, putting nominal tariffs on a few Chinese-manufactured products. He never proposed any serious legislation, though, to actually change the neoliberal trade policies put into place by Reagan/Bush/Clinton.

Sadly, enough Americans believed that professional grifter to get him into the White House (with a little help from Russian oligarchs), but the principle remains: even Republican voters are disgusted by this crisis of corruption that always accompanies neoliberal policies.

Trump then went on the biggest deregulation and tax-cut binge since George W. Bush and Ronald Reagan, passing out over a trillion dollars to the morbidly rich just in 2017 as the opening to what would become a $20.9 trillion tax cut over the following two decades.[1]

He pushed through the Economic Growth, Regulatory Relief, and Consumer Protection Act, which completely screwed consumers and dismantled most of the few good things in Dodd-Frank. He signed more than 100 executive orders, gutting remaining protections for labor, deregulating fossil fuel companies and utilities, gutting public housing, and replacing welfare with "workfare."

Milton Friedman would have been proud.

CHAPTER 13

Biden Challenges Neoliberalism's Core Concepts

When President Joe Biden took office in January 2021, he left in place Trump's few tariffs, which surprised a lot of observers. He followed up by joining with anti-neoliberalism progressives like Senator Bernie Sanders (I-VT) to push for a $3.5 trillion package that would have given Americans free community college; let Medicare negotiate drug prices while expanding its reach to hearing, vision, and dental coverage; and provided 12 weeks of paid family leave, funded by the federal government.

Two bought-off Democratic senators, Kyrsten Sinema of Arizona and Joe Manchin of West Virginia, along with 100 percent of the bought-off Republicans in Congress, killed every one of those provisions, which had over 80 percent popularity.[1]

After more than 30 years of continuous voter opposition to neoliberalism, the Biden administration—if they can hang on to power—may finally signal a real turn back to traditional American policies.

CHAPTER 14

How Neoliberalism Changed America in 40 Years

Under neoliberalism everyone has to negotiate their fate alone, bearing full responsibility for problems that are often not of their own doing. The implications politically, economically and socially for young people are disastrous and are contributing to the emergence of a generation of young people who will occupy a space of social abandonment and terminal exclusion.

—Henry Giroux[1]

Taxes

Neoliberalism dictates that income taxes are a drag on an economy because they limit the money that high-income earners can take and then spend to "create jobs" and "stimulate the economy" with their purchases.

Reality has proven this to be patent nonsense: the period of the greatest growth of the US economy in its history was the period from 1940 to 1981, when income taxes topped out at 91 percent. Every decade since then has seen slower GDP growth than during that 40-year period.

When rich people take in obscene amounts of money, they don't buy extra jeans or cars or TVs: they save it, put it into the stock market, or hide it in overseas tax havens. This actually *does* act as a drag on the economy, as that money, back when it was going instead to middle-class earners with good union jobs, *was* being spent on goods in the economy but is now no longer in circulation.

When Ronald Reagan came into office, the top tax bracket in the United States was 74 percent on the highest-income earners. It acted both as a brake on the accumulation of great wealth (we had no billionaires then) and as a stabilizer for the overall economy.

It also helped maintain high wages for the middle class, as the senior managers of companies were restrained in how much they could personally extract from the corporation, so more was left for good wages.

Reagan dropped that 74 percent bracket all the way down to 25 percent, and today it's in the mid–30 percent range.

The top tax bracket really needs to be above 50 percent if it's to stabilize the economy and prevent huge accumulations of wealth at the top, as economist Thomas Piketty and others have observed watching European nations experiment with neoliberal tax cuts.

Trade

Neoliberalism dictates that the best way to achieve world peace is to interlock national economies through free trade policies dictated by corporations collaboratively with governments.

This is not a new idea. Herbert Spencer, in 1882, wrote,

*While hostile relations with adjacent societies continue,
each society has to be productively self-sufficing; but with
the establishment of peaceful relations, this need for self-
sufficingness ceases. As the local divisions composing
one of our great nations, had, while they were at feud, to
produce each for itself almost everything it required, but
now permanently at peace with one another, have become
so far mutually dependent that no one of them can satisfy
its wants without aid from the rest; so the great nations
themselves, at present forced in large measure to maintain
their economic autonomies, will become less forced to do
this as war decreases, and will gradually become necessary
to one another.*[2]

Neoliberals like Thomas Friedman, Bill Clinton, and Lawrence Summers sold us free trade on the promise that it would
cause China and other repressive regimes to liberalize their
policies and embrace freedom of speech and political activity.

As President Clinton said when the House of Representatives passed his bill to open free trade to China in May 2000:

*If the Senate votes as the House has just done, to extend
permanent normal trade relations with China, it will open
new doors of trade for America and new hope for change
in China. . . . We will be exporting, however, more than our
products. By this agreement, we will also export more of one
of our most cherished values, economic freedom.*

   *Bringing China into the WTO and normalizing trade
will strengthen those who fight for the environment, for*

labor standards, for human rights, for the rule of law. . . .
[T]he more China liberalizes its economy, the more it will
liberate the potential of its people to work without restraint,
to live without fear."[3]

In fact, free trade has done the exact opposite. It's weakened democratic nations like the United States and much of Western Europe while transferring trillions in wealth to China, Vietnam, and other repressive nations whose leaders have used that money to increase the power and efficiency of their internal state security systems. (I cover this in detail in *The Hidden History of Big Brother in America.*)

In 2001, China's GDP was around $2 trillion. That year, President George W. Bush pushed hard for China to be admitted into the World Trade Organization (WTO) so that American companies could use cheap Chinese labor; it was admitted in December of that year. By 2005, its GDP was at $3 trillion; it hit $5 trillion in 2010, $10 trillion in 2015, and today is over $17 trillion and expected to overtake the US in 2022.

As BBC Economics Editor Faisal Islam wrote last year, "China now accounts for 57% of world [steel] production" and has become the world's *leading* producer of everything from ceramic tile to textiles to toys to furniture to advanced electronics.[4]

Free trade has also put democratic nations at the mercy of these autocracies, any one of which could today inflict considerable economic (and thus political) damage on the US and other Western democracies simply by withholding the goods we buy from them.

Health Care

A core tenet of neoliberalism is that of "rugged individualism": the individual citizen shouldn't need help of any sort from government, because the magic free market will meet all needs in ways that perfectly match the needs, rights, and worthiness of the individual.

As Margaret Thatcher famously pointed out, neoliberals don't believe there's any such thing as "society," but only a collection of individuals and their families.

Since government shouldn't be supporting the needs of citizens for health care and shouldn't be "interfering" with the health insurance market by regulating it, neoliberal political policies since the Reagan Revolution have decimated Americans' access to affordable health care.

In the early 1970s, before Reagan, I was a partner in a small herbal tea company. We had 18 employees at our peak, and we gave them all full health insurance coverage through Blue Cross/Blue Shield. My recollection is that it cost around $30 per employee per month; my number may be off, but it was easily affordable as an employer.

And the coverage was comprehensive. State law in Michigan at that time required all hospitals and all health insurance companies to be not-for-profit corporations, so instead of trying to earn profits for shareholders, most of this top end of the health care industry was very affordable.

Neoliberal Reaganism took a meat-ax to the entire system. Hospitals are now profit centers and increasingly function as monopolies, and health insurance companies spit out billions in profits every quarter. And average families are screwed if or when somebody gets sick.

We have over a half-million bankruptcies in the US caused by medical debt every year. In Canada that number is *zero*. It's also zero for every major democracy in Europe and all of Scandinavia.

Education and Higher Education

Neoliberalism argues that "individual responsibility" is the highest value in society, and therefore students and their families should pay for their education. If those families can't afford to pay for school, their children should pursue vocations that don't require education or go to the free market for a loan.

I went to college briefly in the late 1960s and paid for my tuition, books, and rent with a part-time job weekdays pumping gas and changing tires at an Esso station on Trowbridge Road in East Lansing, Michigan, and a Saturday job as a dishwasher at the Bob's Big Boy restaurant across the street from the gas station.

The only person I knew then who had student loans was a friend who was working on his master's degree. Several friends moved out to California because that state's university system was almost entirely free of tuition.

Today, because of neoliberal policies starting in the 1980s, we have almost $2 trillion in student debt in America, a phenomenon you won't find in any other developed country in the world. Even Costa Rica offers free or nearly free college to its young people.[5] After all, that's the future of the nation!

Meanwhile, neoliberals in America are still working as hard as they can to provide "alternatives" to public schools so that upper-middle-class kids can go to private academies while public schools become dumping grounds for poor students (both grade-wise and family-income-wise, and those reinforce each other in a downward spiral).

Finance

Neoliberalism says that markets must be free of government interference to operate efficiently, and finance is the first among those many markets.

Ending the 1933 Glass-Steagall Act, which kept banks honest, was a major project that neoliberals accomplished in 1999: their theory was that if any individual banks became "bad actors," then public opprobrium and shame would force them to change their ways.

In fact, when the predicted banking crisis happened in 2008 at the end of the Bush administration, it took literally trillions of dollars out of the public till and from the Federal Reserve to prevent the entire world's economic system from freezing up and then melting down.

Hundreds of billions of those dollars found their way into the pockets and personal offshore accounts of thousands of those bankers, who continue to engage in massive high-interest-rate rip-offs, particularly of low- and middle-income people.

Employment

Neoliberalism views wages as just another piece of the mosaic that makes up an economy. Any government involvement in wages, be it setting minimum wages or protecting workers' right to unionize, is a "market interference" that will, they say, produce market dislocations and thus diminish freedom.

Here in the real world, about two-thirds of all jobs in America when Reagan took office in 1981 were "living wage" jobs. A third of American workers had union protections, and another third got pretty much the same wages and benefits because their employers had to compete with union shops for workers.

Reagan went to war with unions, and by the end of the Reagan/Bush/Clinton 1980–2001 era, we lost all but about 6 percent of unionized jobs in the private sector.

Arguably, today that means that only 12 percent of American workers have living-wage jobs. While the actual number is higher, we've seen how the middle class ceased to be in the middle around 2015, when more than half of American workers were earning a "middle class" wage.

Similarly, neoliberals believe that minimum wages are inappropriate interferences in the free market, which is why today's $7.25 federal minimum wage is, in inflation-adjusted dollars, actually several dollars lower than the purchasing power of the 1980 minimum wage.

The trend line—interrupted by the dislocation of the pandemic but still generally on track unless or until union protections are restored by law—continues toward replacing the American middle class with a working class hanging on to their lifestyle and their future by their fingernails.

Homelessness

Because neoliberalism views everything in a marketplace as having essentially equal value and weight to everything else, essential human needs like housing are just another market element subject to the whims and manipulations of the free market.

Even the protection of housing from speculation—particularly by foreign actors and international hedge funds based in New York—is considered a market interference.

The result, since the early 1980s, has been an explosion in the cost of housing, pushing more and more Americans out of the possibility of building wealth/equity by owning their homes and instead making them subject to the caprices of landlords.

Much of the damage of these policies has been moderated by the Fed keeping interest rates low since the multiple neoliberalism-caused recessions of the 2001 dot-com bubble bursting, the 2008 housing market meltdown, and the 2019 COVID recession.

Nonetheless, America has seen a storm of homelessness characteristic of countries going through neoliberal transitions. I traveled through Poland, Latvia, Estonia, and Lithuania in the first year after the breakup of the Soviet Union and still remember sitting in an outdoor café in Warsaw as person after person, many of them elderly, came up offering to sell us household goods, sometimes in exchange for the food we were eating.

One particularly poignant moment was when an elderly woman offered to sell Louise and me her deceased husband's tray of World War II medals for $5. It was heartbreaking, but no different than what's happening today in much of America because of 40 years of softer and slower but still relentless neoliberal policies.

Inflation

In *The Hidden History of Monopolies: How Big Business Destroyed the American Dream*, I point out how American families pay, on average, $5,000 a year more than families in Canada and Europe for basic things like telephone service, access to the internet, pharmaceuticals, air travel, and even hotels and restaurants.

The reason is simple. Neoliberalism says there should be no limits on corporate activity or size because the free market will magically regulate everything.

As a result, in the early 1980s, Reagan essentially told his Department of Justice, Federal Trade Commission, and Securities and Exchange Commission to stop enforcing the nation's antitrust and antimonopoly laws regulating corporate mergers and acquisitions.

This period, corporate America's Wild West, was referred to as the era of "mergers and acquisitions mania," and people like Michael Milken, "M&A artists," were lionized in the press, movies, and pop culture.

Before that time, every city in America had its own character because most everything from the local bank to the restaurants and hotels was locally owned. There might be a big retailer like Sears that anchored the local strip mall, but most of the stores were either locally owned or owned by in-state companies.

Today, you could parachute out of a plane and land in any city in America—big, medium-sized, or small—and have no idea where you were. The Olive Gardens, TGI Fridays, Wells Fargos, Marriotts, Home Depots, Walmarts, and Staples stores are all the same everywhere.

And because these companies have such market dominance and have destroyed their smaller competitors with impunity, they can charge pretty much whatever they want. Which, as Clinton Labor Secretary Robert Reich pointed out in November 2021, drove substantial inflation in the US in 2021 as these giants exploited temporary shortages while the economy recovered from COVID.[6]

Because one of the major selling points of neoliberalism is that it can fight inflation, neoliberals like Lawrence Summers and other similarly discredited economists are recommending more neoliberalism, more deregulation, to deal with today's inflation. What a surprise!

Media and News

Prior to neoliberalism in America, media and news had a special place in the laws and policies of our country. Since Thomas Jefferson wrote that newspapers were more important than governments because a free and democratic society cannot exist without a free press, laws were put in place to keep our press free and our news organizations responsive to their communities.

I worked in radio news in the late 1960s and early 1970s in Lansing, Michigan. The Fairness Doctrine and Equal Time Rule required that any statements made on our air by station management that involved politics or public policy had to be balanced by a statement from a member of the community with an opposite or different position.

We were required to "program in the public interest," and that was a critical requirement for our annual station license renewal; radio and TV stations met that standard by offering news at the top of every hour on radio and for an hour in primetime TV.

Every radio station in Lansing at that time was locally owned because the telecommunications laws limited ownership of newspapers and of radio and TV stations to local people and had strict rules against any one family or company owning too much of the media in any particular market or state.

ABC, CBS, and NBC all lost money every year on their news operations and had bureaus across the country and all over the world. Those losses were the cost of doing business, the price they paid to program in the public interest and be allowed to carry their entertainment programming and advertising into millions of homes every day and night.

Today, since Reagan stopped enforcing the Fairness Doctrine in 1987 and Obama eliminated it from telecom law altogether during his presidency, none of the stations in Lansing are owned by a local family or company (as far as I can find with an internet search).

News for the big three networks has become a profit center, and cable competitors are similarly motivated by the constant search for profits. More than half of the newspapers in America are owned by hedge funds, and their newsrooms have been gutted.[7]

When Clinton signed the Telecommunications Act of 1996, he ended local ownership rules and overall antimonopoly ownership regulations nationally. Within a few years, giants like Clear Channel and Cumulus had accumulated thousands of stations nationwide and programmed hundreds of them with right-wing talk radio pushing a neoliberal line.

News has become a never-ending search for the next scandal or salacious story; the old axiom "If it bleeds, it leads" has become gospel, and Americans are among the most poorly informed people in the developed world. But the purveyors of what's left of our news infrastructure are getting rich.

The Environment

Neoliberalism considers the value of the environment only so far as it interacts with the free market.

Everything in the neoliberal universe is reducible to dollars and cents, so environmental destruction that doesn't produce harm to the economy is inconsequential. It's why there's such a big fight over the protection of our natural environment and culturally significant Native American sites.

In the neoliberal world, if the environment is ravaged by carbon or other pollution, any mitigation has to be weighed on a cost-benefit scale without consideration of the beauty, wonder, or cultural meaning of the natural world. Even worse, future harms—like global warming or abandoned wells and mines—are considered irrelevant because they don't have immediate economic impacts. If it can't be bought and sold, it's of no value and not worth protecting, particularly if by exploiting or destroying it somebody can make a buck.

Neoliberalism almost never considers the future; it's very much a here-and-now worldview. The old Iroquois idea of making decisions in the context of their impact on the "seventh generation" (the seven generations were great-grandma, grandma, this generation, daughter, granddaughter, great-granddaughter and great-great-granddaughter) is inconceivable to the neoliberal way of thinking.

Neoliberalism is always reactive rather than proactive. If a harm is committed, neoliberals say, it can be remedied through actions in the courts or public shame. But preventing a harm like Big Fossil Fuel devastating the atmosphere or Big Ag poisoning our food supply just to increase profits is not the job of government.

CHAPTER 15

Privatizing
the Commons

It happened 56 years *before* Benjamin Franklin walked out of Independence Hall in Philadelphia and told Elizabeth Willing Powel, the wife of Philadelphia's mayor and one of the most influential women in the nation, that they had just created "a republic, if you can keep it."[1]

On July 1, 1731, Franklin and his 12 Junto Club associates incorporated the nation's first public library. At the time, most books were imported and extraordinarily expensive, but Franklin and his associates believed the effort would pay off for the nation.[2]

"[T]hese Libraries have improved the general Conversation of Americans," he wrote in his autobiography, "made the common Tradesmen and Farmers as intelligent as most Gentlemen from other Countries, and perhaps have contributed in some Degree to the Stand so generally made throughout the Colonies in Defence of their Priviledges."[3]

Public libraries caught on and spread across the nation; literacy and thoughtful political debate followed them.

And now neoliberal parasites are trying to turn these public goods into profit centers for Wall Street through privatization.

Librarian and author Caleb Nichols has written over at Truthout.org about Library Systems and Services [LS&S], "a for-profit, private company that has been quietly infiltrating public libraries since 1997."[4] This is the latest alarming part of a larger trend. As the Volcker Alliance found in a 2015 report, over 40 percent of people doing the government's work are actually employed by private business.[5]

This privatization binge started in America during the Reagan administration, when Republicans embraced neoliberalism instead of classical economics and committed to turning all government functions over to their wealthy private-sector donors.

Ridiculing and slandering those who devoted their lives to the service of their country, Reagan cynically proclaimed, "The best minds are not in government. If any were, business would steal them away."

But privatization is one of the biggest cons ever perpetrated on the American people, run not by "the *best* minds" but by the *greediest*.

Their sales pitch is that if government will use its extraordinary and singular power to tax people, and then hand that money over to private corporations, those corporations will serve the public better and cheaper than the government could do. The main way companies that prey on tax dollars do this is by paying their workers crap wages after they've voided union contracts, slashed benefits, and ended pensions.

The result is devastating to communities, while the services—something we see vividly with all the scandals around privatized prisons, power companies, and schools—are substandard and no longer accountable to public scrutiny.

When local services are privatized and wages slashed, the good pay that used to recirculate in the community now goes as profits to a distant city where the privatizing corporation is headquartered, or even overseas into tax shelters for the privatizing company and its senior executives.

Because public-sector government jobs often define the "good job floor" for local wages and benefits, other local employers follow suit and cut wages and benefits, further devastating local economies. After widespread privatization, poverty creeps across communities like a slow-spreading but relentless fungus.

Many of these privatized workers now qualify for public benefits like food stamps and Medicaid as well as local forms of assistance, subsidizing the corporation while draining even more resources from the community and government. As reported in *In the Public Interest*: "A 2009 study on the effects of outsourcing on food service workers in K–12 public schools in New Jersey found that companies such as Aramark, Sodexo, and Compass cut workers' wages by $4–$6 per hour following privatization. Many workers completely lost their health insurance benefits. [Now] food service contractors have the highest level of employees and their children enrolled in New Jersey FamilyCare, the state's Medicaid program."[6]

With impoverished workers spending less money in the local economy, small businesses struggle to survive and are more easily pushed out by giant concerns that promise jobs but demand millions in tax breaks and abatements, a process called "Wal-Martization."

That, in turn, cuts tax revenues that support local government entities—particularly schools, libraries, and police and fire departments—making them even more reliant on their corporate predator "partners" who will eventually say, "You can't afford the payments any longer, so just give us the whole thing."

These firms also hide behind the veil of "trade secrets" and the Fourth Amendment "right of privacy" (corporations are people too, according to five conservatives on the Supreme Court) to keep reporters and citizens from knowing what they're doing to screw these communities out of their tax dollars.

Not only is the public blocked from knowing what their governments are agreeing to as public functions are privatized, but government itself (outside of those signing the initial contracts before moving on to well-paid jobs in the private sector) is often forbidden to know the details.

As Morgan Smith wrote in a 2013 *New York Times* article titled "When Private Firms Run Schools, Financial Secrecy Is Allowed," "On a recently approved Texas charter school application, blacked-out paragraphs appear on almost 100 of its 393 pages."[7]

When newspapers sue under the Freedom of Information Act, which is supposed to keep government activities transparent to the taxpayers who fund them, they're simply turned away, as the *Times* article noted: "When the *Texas Tribune* made an open-records request for employee salary records and marketing expenses at the state's [privatized] full-time virtual schools, it received responses from all but one of those connected with for-profit entities indicating either that the records were not available or were not subject to public information laws."[8]

Even worse, government agencies that do have oversight powers usually don't have the additional personnel required to provide oversight and regulation of these private compa-nies in those few cases where they're not blocked by confiden-tiality contracts.

Thus, billions are routinely stolen by the companies, and governments only discover it (if at all) long after the CEOs have stashed the money in their offshore tax havens.

As Rutgers researcher Patrice M. Mareschal found, "Our review of contractor oversight in New Jersey shows that the state is failing in its duty of protecting vulnerable citizens from poor service and taxpayers from wasted funds. At the core of the problem is a complete lack of priority given to oversight despite a preference for contracted service provision. This is best exemplified by the massive shortage in qualified staff to manage contracts."[9]

Not only that, but private corporations can get away with behaviors that are imprisonable crimes when committed by government employees. These now-legal breaches of the public trust include self-dealing, handing off cash to fam-ily members, paying off politicians, and harassing or firing whistleblowers.

According to a report for the Colorado Center for Pol-icy Studies, "[P]rivate providers are generally not subject to conflict-of-interest laws, nepotism statutes or ordinances, eth-ics codes or whistleblower protection for their employees, or restrictions on political involvement. This last omission makes it possible to use political influence to get contracts and to increase public demand for their services. A prime example of this has been the large corporations that build, own, or man-age prisons."[10]

Those private prison companies, of course, lobby politicians for harsher laws and longer jail terms for offenders, even working against efforts to decriminalize marijuana, all to increase their incarcerated populations and thus their profits. It is not a coincidence that as prisons became privatized, the rates of incarceration rose and the prisons filled up with new customers—the formerly working poor.

The goal here is to convert as much public tax money to private profit as possible, and they use a lot of fancy language and slick formulas to make it happen.

For example, Senators Rob Portman (R-OH) and Joe Manchin slipped a little-known "value for money" stipulation into the $1.2 trillion Bipartisan Infrastructure bill that passed in 2021, essentially turning almost every dollar in it over to private-sector corporations as "public-private partnerships." Screwing the public like this is what got them enough Republican votes for the bill to pass the Senate.

"Public-private partnerships are valuable ways for states and localities to complete projects through financially sound solutions," Manchin bragged in a press release. "Our bipartisan legislation will require states and communities to consider public-private partnerships when reviewing transportation project financing to ensure that we are making the best use of taxpayer dollars."[11]

It doesn't even make sense. If a government agency can do something for, say, $100 million, how could a private corporation do it for less when they have to skim 30 percent, or $30 million, off the top for their own profits, shareholder dividends, and absurd CEO and senior executive pay?

At the same time that Reagan was pitching privatization of public services, he was also pushing the idea that Americans were rugged individualists who should take care of their own families and communities. But how do you take care of your own community when it's turned its tax dollars and functions over to a private corporation owned by a Wall Street hedge fund whose executives stash their money in foreign tax shelters?

Ben Franklin isn't the only Founder who must be rolling over in his grave (Jefferson, for example, created the University of Virginia as a "free forever" college), and the legacy of Franklin's libraries isn't the only loss to our society as corporations eat our public sectors alive.

It's hard to find a single aspect of government, from federal to state to local, that hasn't been touched by this cancer.

Unemployment and "food stamp" programs now run with fee-based cards from Wall Street banks, toll roads and parking meters are owned by foreign corporations, and even our military and intelligence agencies are deeply infected with this curse (Edward Snowden, who spilled the National Security Agency's secrets, worked for a private corporate defense contractor).

The Reason Foundation, an outgrowth of the Koch brothers' efforts, points out proudly how huge this process has become, even arguing for privatizing fire departments across the nation.[12] (Franklin also started Philadelphia's first fire department.)

And now they're after our libraries. As Caleb Nichols notes in his Truthout article, "Flexing into a new type of market, the sky is apparently the limit for LS&S [Library Systems and Services], which according to its own website has shockingly morphed into 'the 3rd largest library system in the United States.'"[13]

The result of privatizing libraries will, no doubt, be the same as what has followed the privatizing of hundreds of other government functions since Reagan. Again, Nichols nails it about this corporation, which itself is owned by a private equity company: "When companies like LS&S privatize public goods, old contracts—and unions—are thrown out. Workers, even PMC workers like degreed librarians, cease earning annual salaries, solid benefits and government-backed pensions, and are instead given comparably lower hourly wages, private retirement accounts, and have no collective bargaining power or ability to file grievances. LS&S claims to be a public good—by saving communities taxpayer money—but it is actually destroying good-paying, union-backed jobs and paving the way for more private takeovers of public goods."[14]

The 40-year experiment with the neoliberal/Republican/corporate takeover of government functions at all levels has impoverished communities across America while filling the money bins of politically connected and morbidly rich CEOs of these public-private partnership scams.

Now it's threatening to turn Ben Franklin's public libraries into corporate profit centers.

Destruction of Democracy

Neoliberalism argues that governments should be largely passive players in the lives of their citizens, merely providing basic services like a military to protect the nation and police to protect the streets. Beyond that, politicians should simply say no to any government efforts to improve the lives of average Americans.

As a result, the entire Republican Party, which is still all in on neoliberalism, and a sizable remnant of Clinton's neoliberal faction within the Democratic Party have fought any sort of major government efforts to maintain or improve national infrastructure ("It should be a 'local responsibility'") or provide for the needs of working-class people (as noted earlier).

Well over 50 percent of the American people—often polls show support as high as 90 percent—want things that Canadian, European, and Japanese citizens have, like free or low-cost health care, free or low-cost college, good schools, modern mass transit, and the regulation of predatory corporate behavior.

In every instance since the Reagan Revolution, the entire GOP has fought every such effort, and in many cases they've been joined by bought-off Democrats claiming that "liberals" are "too extreme" for "center-right America."

Voters across the political spectrum know their politicians have been ignoring them while serving the needs and desires of big corporations and the morbidly rich since the 1980s. Our political response to this has been cynicism and anger, causing some Americans to check out of political involvement, while others have taken to the streets and even tried to seize the US Capitol.

People feel like democracy has failed them—and, in reality, it has. But it happened by intent. When Ronald Reagan said that government was the cause of, not the solution to, our problems, he believed that bit of neoliberal doctrine. The same was true when Bill Clinton declared an end to the era of welfare and "big government."

The founders of neoliberalism had seen governments become so powerful that they turned into tyrannical fascist and communist states: they were determined that no democracy should ever again vote an Adolf Hitler into office.

Therefore, weakening democracy itself is at the core of neoliberal policy. If big corporations or entire industries like pharma or insurance want to buy a particular politician, neoliberals on the Supreme Court declared in *Citizens United v. Federal Election Commission* in 2010, that's no longer bribery or political corruption: it's free speech and protected by the First Amendment to the Constitution.

The Biden administration has worked mightily to reverse this trend and show Americans that government can, once again after four decades, work for the great mass of the people. Whether they'll be able to overcome their neoliberal opposition in both parties is still an open question.

Breaking with 40 Years of Neoliberalism

A little fact is as important as what is called a big fact.
The picture may be well-nigh finished, but it remains vague for
want of one more fact. When that missing fact is discovered,
all others become clear and distinct; it is like turning a light,
properly shaded, upon a painting which but a moment before
was a blur in the dimness. . . . Facts when justly arranged
interpret themselves. They tell the story.

—**Albert J. Beveridge, biographer of Abraham Lincoln**[1]

Undoing 40-plus years of neoliberal tax, trade, and social policies won't happen overnight and will cause considerable turmoil, particularly for the very rich.

That said, it'll be incredibly popular, as the populist presidential campaigns of both Bernie Sanders and Donald Trump proved.

Right now, neoliberalism is in transition, as its corruption and the method by which it increases inequality, by pushing money to the very few at the top of the economic pyramid, are increasingly visible and unpopular.

One way it may survive in America is to follow the path it took in Russia and Hungary, where neoliberal policies produced an oligarchic class that seized control of the government itself. President Vladimir Putin and Prime Minister

Viktor Orbán both then put their cronies in charge of most major industries, took control of the media, empowered their intelligence and police agencies to crush dissent, and turned their democracies into a hollow shell, a Potemkin village, that looks like a democracy from the outside but very much is not on the inside.

I detail how this process works and how it could play out in America in *The Hidden History of American Oligarchy*. Neoliberal corporate policy also inevitably leads to an explosion of monopoly, an issue I've explored in depth in *The Hidden History of Monopolies*.

Because those two previous books in this series do such deep dives into oligarchy and monopoly, I won't delve further into them in this book. But they're just the visible part of the iceberg; underneath are the two main policies used by neoliberals to consolidate wealth and break the back of labor, transforming both the American economy and our society— neoliberal *tax* and *trade* policy—so it's worth examining both in some detail.

CHAPTER 18

#TaxTheRich

Forty years of neoliberalism has collapsed the American middle class, and neoliberal tax policy had a lot to do with it.

Seven years ago, the American middle class ceased to be more than half of us: the middle class went from two-thirds of Americans when Reagan took office in 1981 to 49 percent in 2015. National Public Radio commemorated it with the headline, "The Tipping Point: Most Americans No Longer Are Middle Class."[1]

In 2021, according to the US Census and the Federal Reserve, "middle class" households sank below the top 1 percent in total wealth: a handful of superrich households now have more wealth than the entire American middle class. The headline went to *Bloomberg*: "Top 1% of U.S. Earners Now Hold More Wealth Than All of the Middle Class."[2]

CHAPTER 19

Rebuilding a Middle Class Gutted by Neoliberalism

There's nothing normal about having a middle class.

Having a middle class is a choice that a society has to make, and it's a choice we need to make again in this generation if we want to stop the neoliberal destruction of the remnants of the last generation's middle class.

Despite what you might read in the *Wall Street Journal* or see on Fox "News," neoliberal capitalism is not an economic system that naturally produces a middle class. In fact, if left to its own devices, neoliberal capitalism *always* causes vast levels of inequality while aggravating the problem of corporate monopoly.[1]

The natural and most stable state of capitalism actually looks a lot like the Victorian England depicted in Charles Dickens's novels. Here's how it works:

In a classic unregulated neoliberal economy like the one, for example, in Dickens's 1843 novel *A Christmas Carol*, there is, at the top, a very small class of the superrich. In Dickens's time, that was the British royal family, wealthy industrialists, and the owners of banks, shipping firms, and the like.

Below them, there is a slightly larger, but still very small, "middle" class of professionals and merchants—doctors, lawyers, shop owners—who help keep things running for the superrich and supply the working poor with their needs. In Dickens's novel, Ebenezer Scrooge was in this class.

And at the very bottom there is the great mass of people—typically over 90 percent of the population—who make up the working poor. They have no wealth—in fact, they're typically in debt all of their lives—and can barely survive on what little money they make. That's Bob Cratchit, his son Tiny Tim, and the rest of the Cratchit family.

So, for average working people, there is no option of getting into the *middle* class in neoliberal unregulated capitalism. Wealth accumulates at the very top among the elites, not among everyday working people, who remain the working poor and can't even build equity through home ownership.

This kind of inequality is the default option of capitalism unless it's regulated to establish and maintain a middle class that extends beyond professionals and small-business owners.

You can see this trend today in stark relief. When we had heavily regulated and taxed capitalism in the post–World War II era, the largest employer in America was General Motors, and it paid working people what would be, in today's dollars, about $50 an hour with benefits.

President Reagan began deregulating labor markets and cutting taxes in 1981, and today, with neoliberal "raw capitalism"—what many call "Reaganomics"—in place, our nation's largest employer is Walmart, and it pays an average of around $13 an hour.[2]

This is how quickly capitalism reorients itself when the brakes of regulation and taxes are removed by neoliberal policies: this huge change was accomplished in less than 40 years.

The only ways in which a *workers'* middle class can come about in a capitalist society are by massive social upheaval causing a widespread worker shortage—a middle class emerged after the Black Plague killed off a third of the labor force in Europe in the 14th century—or by regulating labor markets (healthy minimum wage, union protections) and heavily taxing the rich.

French economist Thomas Piketty wrote about this at great length in his groundbreaking book *Capital in the Twenty-First Century*. He argued that the middle class that came about in Western Europe and the United States during the mid-20th century was the direct result of a peculiar set of moments in history that empowered labor, combined with high levels of taxation on the very rich.[3]

According to Piketty, the post–World War II European middle class was created by two major events: the destruction of European inherited wealth during the war and higher taxes imposed on the rich, most of which were necessitated by the war. This combination, along with a strong labor movement that emerged across Europe after the war, held down wealth and income at the top and raised up working people into a middle class.

Progressive taxation, when done correctly, pushes wages in the direction of working people and reduces the incentives for the very rich to pillage their companies or rip off their workers. After all, why take another billion when 91 percent of it is just going to be paid in taxes?

This is the main reason why, when General Motors was our largest employer and our working class were also in the middle class, CEOs took home only 30 times what working people did. The top tax rate for all the time that America's middle class was created (1933–1981) was between 74 and 91 percent. Until, of course, Reagan dropped it to 25 percent and began the process of shifting working people out of the middle class and into the category of the working poor.

Other policies, such as protective tariffs and strong labor laws, also help build a middle class, but progressive taxation is the most important because it is the most direct way to transfer money from the rich to the government programs that provide a social-safety-net "floor" for the working poor; and, most important, it creates a disincentive to theft or monopoly by those at the top.

History shows how important high taxes on the rich are for creating a strong middle class. The period with the highest taxes on the rich—the period between the Roosevelt and Reagan administrations—was also the period with the lowest levels of economic inequality and the greatest growth in the US economy.

Ever since marginal tax rates started to plummet during the Reagan years, income inequality has skyrocketed and the US economy has never, in any decade since 1980, reached the levels of sustained growth that it saw during the period from 1930 to 1980.

Even more striking, during those same 40 years since Reagan took office and started cutting taxes on the rich, income levels for the top 1 percent ballooned, while income levels for everyone else stayed pretty much flat.

Coincidence? Not a chance: this is how deregulated or neoliberal capitalism normally works: eating the middle class and burping what's left of their wealth up to the very rich.

Creating a middle class is always a choice, and by embracing neoliberal Reaganomics and cutting taxes on the rich, we decided, back in 1981, not to have a majority of workers in the middle class within a generation or two.

As I noted in *The Hidden History of American Oligarchy*, there is a reason why conservative politicians always, throughout history, have pushed for neoliberal-type policies: by keeping working-class people impoverished, they minimize labor strikes and reduce the ability of working people to demand a share of the economic pie.

Conservatives—all the way back to their opposition to the American Revolution in 1776—have always advocated the class interests of the rich over working people. *Always*. From David Hume (1700s) to John C. Calhoun (1800s) to today's Republican Party. It's a functional description of *conservative*.

Conservatives know that when wealth is spread more equally among all parts of society, working-class people start to expect more from society and start demanding more rights. Social and worker movements emerge with actual power behind them because people are no longer impoverished.

That leads to "social instability," which is feared and hated by conservatives, even though America's history shows that such instability got us nearly all of our significant progressive movements, from the abolition of slavery to voting rights for women and African Americans to the right to unionize.

This empowerment of previously marginalized working-class people is exactly what happened in the 1960s and '70s when taxes on the rich were at their highest. The civil rights movement, the women's movement, the consumer movement, the antiwar movement, the gay marriage/rights movement, and the environmental movement—social movements that grew out of the wealth and rising expectations of the post–World War II era's middle class—all terrified conservatives.

Which is why ever since they took power in 1980, conservative Republicans have made ripping working people out of the middle class and turning them into a more compliant class of the working poor their number one goal.

We now have to make a choice in this country.

We can either continue going down the road to neoliberal oligarchy—absolute rule by the rich, the road we've been on since the Reagan years—or choose to return to FDR's Keynesian economics, raise taxes on the rich, reverse free trade, and create a more pluralistic society where working-class people are able to make it into the middle class.

We can't have both neoliberal tax policies and a majority of Americans in the middle class: they're mutually exclusive.

CHAPTER 20

Trade: Returning to Alexander Hamilton's American Plan

The issue of trade goes way, way back, and it's important to understand its history if we're going to fix things here today.

Shortly after George Washington was elected president, he tasked his secretary of the Treasury, Alexander Hamilton, with figuring out how to turn America into an economic powerhouse that could compete with the giants of Europe. In 1791, Hamilton turned in his *Report on the Subject of Manufactures* (detailed later in this chapter), borrowing heavily from King Henry VII's "Tudor Plan" from the late 15th century.[1]

Henry VII had transformed England from a provincial mud-streets, thatched-roofs backwater whose main product was wool into an industrial powerhouse by *encouraging* exports of finished goods while using taxes to *discourage* the import of any finished goods that competed with products manufactured in England.

English traders could import raw materials to be transformed into finished goods in England's early factories with virtually no import/export taxes (they're called tariffs), and they could ship out finished products all over the world, again with no tariffs. Cheap raw materials came into the country, English workers were paid a good wage to convert them into expensive finished products, and those products were then sold around the world. All with no tariffs. The profit from converting raw materials into finished goods was shared between the English workers and the factory owners: it turned England into one of the world's wealthiest nations in a few generations.

On the domestic side, Henry VII encouraged British manufacturing and profits by putting *high* tariffs on the *export* of *raw materials* that could be used by British factories and on the *import* of *finished products* from the rest of Europe that might compete with British-made goods.

British economist Adam Smith explained the process almost 300 years later, in his 1776 book *Wealth of Nations*, when he noted that raw materials modified by human labor—manufacturing—create the foundation for a nation's wealth.

For example, a tree limb lying on the ground is a raw material with little commercial value. But if a workman applies labor to that limb, turning it into an axe handle, it now has value that will last for generations and becomes part of the "wealth of the nation."

Additionally, if that axe handle were to be sold overseas, that money would come back to England from the sale and would thus *continue* to make England one axe handle richer, to be a part of the wealth of England for generations, *even though it had been sold overseas.*

"By preferring the support of domestic to that of foreign industry," Smith wrote, "he [a British merchant] intends only his own security; and by directing that industry in such a manner as its produce may be of the greatest value, he intends only his own gain, and he is in this, as in many other cases, led by an invisible hand to promote an end which was no part of his intention."[2]

It's the single reference in *Wealth of Nations* to the invisible hand and was made in the context of the importance of a nation's businesspeople supporting their own country's manufactured goods rather than buying cheaper stuff from overseas. (F. A. Hayek took that single reference to the invisible hand and turned it into the cornerstone of neoliberalism in multiple books, articles, and speeches. He came up with his own phrase to amplify the idea: he called it "The Spontaneous Order.")

Smith's book was published in 1776, and a bit over a decade later, on April 14, 1789, George Washington was out walking through the fields at Mount Vernon, his home in Virginia, when Charles Thomson, the secretary of the Continental Congress, showed up on horseback. Thomson had a letter for Washington from the president pro tempore of the new, constitutionally created United States Senate, telling Washington that he'd just been elected president and the inauguration was set for April 30 in the nation's capital, New York City.[3]

It created two problems for Washington.

The first was saying goodbye to his 82-year-old mother, which the 57-year-old Washington did that night. She gave him her blessing and told him that it was the last time he'd see her alive, as she was gravely ill, and indeed she died before he returned from New York.

The second was finding a suit of clothes made in America. For that, he sent a courier to his old friend and fellow general from the American Revolutionary War, Henry Knox.

Washington couldn't find a suit made in America because in the years prior to the American Revolution, the British

East India Company (whose tea was thrown into Boston Harbor by outraged colonists after the Tea Act of 1773 gave the world's largest transnational corporation a giant tax break) had controlled the manufacture and transportation of a whole range of goods, including fine clothing. Cotton and wool could be grown and sheared in the colonies but had to be sent to England to be turned into clothes.

This was a routine policy for England and was why, until India achieved its independence in 1947, Mahatma Gandhi (who was assassinated a year later) sat with his spinning wheel for his lectures and spun daily in his own home. It was, like his Salt March, a protest against the colonial practices of England and an entreaty to his fellow Indians to make their own clothes to gain independence from British companies and institutions.

Fortunately for George Washington, an American clothing company had been established on April 28, 1783, in Hartford, Connecticut, by a man named Daniel Hinsdale, and they produced high-quality woollen and cotton clothing and also made things from imported silk.[4] It was to Hinsdale's company that Knox turned, and helped Washington get—in time for his inauguration two weeks later—a nice, but not excessively elegant, brown American-made suit. (He wore British black later for the celebrations and the most famous painting.)

For about 200 years, we understood well the benefits of tariffs, subsidized exports, and protectionist policies in the United States. Had American presidents such as Abraham Lincoln, George Washington, Andrew Jackson, or Ulysses S. Grant applied for IMF loans, they would have been denied: all of them believed in high tariffs and a heavy control of foreign investment, and they considered free trade to be absurd.

But it was another Founding Father—Alexander Hamilton—who knew best how to spawn American industry to make the country independent and competitive. As the nation's first Treasury secretary, Hamilton submitted his *Report on the Subject of Manufactures* in 1791 to the US Congress, outlining the need for our government to foster new industries through "bounties" (subsidies) and subsequently protect them from foreign imports until they became globally competitive.

Additionally, he proposed a road map for American industrial development. These steps included protective tariffs on imports, import bans, subsidies, export bans on selected materials, and the development of product standards.

It was this approach of putting America first that our government followed for most of our history, with average tariffs of 30 to 40 percent through the 19th and 20th centuries. There is no denying that it helped turn America into an industrial and economic juggernaut in the mid-20th century and beyond. The three periods when we radically dropped tariffs—for three years in 1857, for nine years in 1913, and in 1987 by Reagan—were all followed by economic disasters, particularly for small American manufacturers.

The post-Reagan era has been particularly destructive to our economy because not only did we mostly eliminate the tariffs, but we became free trade proponents on the international stage. After Reagan blew out our tariffs in the 1980s, and Clinton kicked the door totally open with the General Agreement on Tariffs and Trade (GATT), NAFTA, and the

WTO, our average tariffs are now around *2 percent*. And the predictable result has been the hemorrhaging of American manufacturing capacity to those countries that do protect their industries through high import tariffs but allow exports on the cheap—particularly China and South Korea.

The irony is that we have abandoned Hamilton's advice—and our own history—while China, South Korea, Japan, and other nations are following his prescriptions and turning into muscular and prosperous economic entities.

It's high time we relearned Alexander Hamilton's lessons for our nation.

The first third of Hamilton's report deals with Jefferson's objections to it (withdrawn later), which were primarily over the subsidies to industry, as Jefferson favored America being an agricultural rather than industrial power in 1791. After that, though, Hamilton gets to the rationale for, and the details of, his 11-point plan to turn America into an industrial power and build a strong manufacturing-based middle class.

CHAPTER 21

What Is
Real Wealth?

First, echoing Adam Smith, Hamilton states that real wealth doesn't exist until somebody makes something. A "service economy" is an oxymoron—if I wash your car in exchange for your mowing my lawn, money is moving around, it's an economy of some sort, but no real and lasting wealth is created.

Only through manufacturing, when $5 worth of iron ore is converted into a $2,000 car door, or $1 worth of raw wool is converted into a $1,000 suit, is real wealth created. Hamilton also notes that people being paid for creating wealth (manufacturing) creates wages, which are the principal engine of demand, which drives an economy. And both come from a generally protectionist foreign trade policy.

In an early version of Keynes, Hamilton observed that when people make things, they also earn money, which will be used to buy more things, thus creating a real economy with things of real value circulating in it. In addition, Hamilton saw a clear government role in fostering manufacturing: not just in subsidizing it until it could compete on its own, but also in crafting a foreign policy that favored the protection of American enterprises.

"'Tis for the United States to consider by what means they can render themselves least dependent" of other nations' manufactures, Hamilton wrote, "on the combinations, right or wrong, of foreign policy."[1]

But there were many voices—the loudest being the young Thomas Jefferson—who argued that instead of becoming an industrial power, we should remain an agricultural nation. Hamilton believed that both were possible and there would even be a desirable synergy between the two. He felt that if America wanted to be competitive, it couldn't just leave it to the free market, at least not until home-grown industries were robust enough to compete on their own in the international marketplace.

Government ought to play a role in fostering a strong industrial base, he argued: "To produce the desirable changes, as early as may be expedient, may therefore require the incitement and patronage of government." In fact, Hamilton believed that success was not possible without government. "To be enabled to contend with success, it is evident that the interference and aid of their own government are indispensable," he wrote.

His reasons were pretty straightforward: it would take government's power to set up a playing field for the game of business where investors who would otherwise be able to make more money overseas would keep their money in the United States. "There are weighty inducements to prefer the employment of capital at home even at less profit, to an investment of it abroad, though with greater gain," he wrote.

CHAPTER 22

Hamilton's 11-Step Plan Worked for 188 Years

Having provided this overview, Hamilton got right to the meat of the matter—his 11-step plan, contained in his *Report on the Subject of Manufactures*.[1] It called for government to take an active role in developing its own industry, in discouraging imports through tariffs and prohibitions, in building transportation routes at home for internal trade, and in subsidizing manufacturing until companies become strong enough to compete on their own.

Hamilton's proposed program was largely implemented by Congress and President Washington by 1793, putting America on course to become the richest country in the history of the world. Hamilton's American Plan included the following:[2]

"Protecting duties—or duties on those foreign articles which are the rivals of the domestic ones, intended to be encouraged."

"Prohibition of rival articles or duties equivalent to prohibitions."

"Prohibitions of the exportation of the materials of manufacturers."

"The exemption of the [raw] materials of manufactures from [import] duty."

A system to regulate the quality of production for export: "Judicious regulations for the inspection of manufactured commodities."

And a banking system and navy to make trade easier and protect vessels at sea.

From 1793 until 1981, Hamilton's system made America—and America's working class—the richest in the world. We imported iron ore from overseas, for example; turned it into steel; made that into cars and washing machines and a million other things; and sold them all over the world. And the money from those exports came back to America, making us richer.

CHAPTER 23

Tariffs Built America

Our tariff system was so successful that it paid 100 percent of the cost of running the US federal government, from the salaries of Congress to the cost of the Army and Navy and everything in between, until the Lincoln administration. From Lincoln to World War I, tariffs paid between two-thirds and one-half of the total cost of government.

It's why we didn't even have an income tax until 1913, outside of a brief period during the Civil War. But the *main* benefit of Hamilton's system wasn't the tariffs' revenue: it was their power to encourage Smith's application of labor to raw materials—manufacturing—that built the "wealth of the nation" of the United States.

Then came Friedman, Hayek, and Mises's neoliberal free trade ideology as the centerpiece of the Reagan Revolution. The CEOs of America's manufacturing companies were looking at the high cost of their mostly unionized American labor force and saying, "But I can get people in Mexico or China to make this same product for $2 an hour or less!"

A major campaign began to "liberalize" American trade policy, complete with think tanks and people like the wealthy *New York Times* columnist Thomas Friedman.[1]

As a result, we've lost over 60,000 factories since the day Reagan was inaugurated. Not jobs—that's in the *tens of millions*, particularly when you count secondary jobs maintained in towns across America by the income of people with good union jobs—that's *factories* that were simply abandoned or moved, brick-by-brick, from the US to Mexico, China, Vietnam, or other low-wage nations.

As the Council on Foreign Relations reported, "U.S. manufacturing employment dropped from 26 percent of the workforce in 1970 to 8.5 percent in 2016."[2]

Keep in mind, manufacturing is the single most effective way to build the wealth of a nation. Even when products are sold overseas, that wealth always comes back home. This is true regardless of the level of automation involved: the country that transforms the cheap raw material into the expensive finished good earns and keeps that profit, or wealth, whether the product is sold domestically or internationally.

When Reagan was sworn into office, Sam Walton's slogan for his Walmart chain was "100% Made In America!" Today, it might as well be, "Nothing but cheap junk made in China, where we send all your wealth except what we can skim off the top!"

But What About the Cost of American-Made Goods?

One of the main arguments brought against rolling back neoliberal free trade policies in the United States is that we've become addicted, essentially, to cheap goods made in low-wage countries.

Because they've so deeply permeated our retail sector, the logic goes, if we bring those factories back to America (or build new ones here), because American labor and American environmental regulations are more costly than in low-wage, poorly regulated nations, the price of everything now coming from China and other low-wage countries will explode.

If labor made up most of the cost of a product, that would be an arguable point. But even in low-wage countries, automation is widespread, and most goods rely more on machines than on hand labor to manufacture products. So the impact of labor costs going up will generally be marginal.

But it will show up; that much was true in 1791 as much as it's true today. And Hamilton had an answer to the naysayers: it will all even out soon enough.

Hamilton wrote in his *Report on the Subject of Manufactures* that "[i]t is not an unreasonable supposition, that measures, which serve to abridge the free competition of foreign Articles, have a tendency to occasion an enhancement of prices and it is not to be denied that such is the effect in a number of Cases; but the fact does not uniformly correspond with the theory."[1]

In fact, Hamilton pointed out, in some cases it may even lower prices, both because of the reduced cost of shipping and also because once goods are made here, those manufacturing enterprises will attract competitors, and that competition will ultimately lower prices.

"A reduction of prices has in several instances immediately succeeded the establishment of a domestic manufacture," he wrote. In fact, lower prices as a result of bringing manufacturing home is an almost universal principle. He went on to say,

> But though it were true, that the immediate and certain effect of regulations controuling [sic] the competition of foreign with domestic fabrics was an increase of price, it is universally true, that the contrary is the ultimate effect with every successful manufacture. When a domestic manufacture has attained to perfection, and has engaged in the prosecution of it a competent number of Persons, it invariably becomes cheaper. Being free from the heavy charges, which attend the importation of foreign commodities, it can be afforded, and accordingly seldom or never fails to be sold Cheaper, in process of time, than was the foreign Article for which it is a substitute. The internal competition, which takes place, soon does away every thing like Monopoly, and by degrees reduces the price of the Article to the minimum of a reasonable profit on the Capital employed [emphasis in the original]. This accords with the reason of the thing and with experience.

Although bringing manufacturing to America would lower the cost of goods over time while simultaneously enriching the country, this is a process that the so-called free market would never bring about, Hamilton observed. The main reason is that there's essentially no such thing as a "free market": every country, from Hamilton's time to today, has its own industrial policy and its own set of rules for trade, including some that even use government funds via bounties and premiums—government subsidies—to develop new products or industries.

Here in America, for example, it was government funding that created the internet and also pays for the lion's share of the development of new classes of pharmaceuticals, among other things. The benefits of the NASA space program of the 1960s, from Velcro to miniaturization of electronics, are famous. These government funds built entire industries.

"It is well known," Hamilton wrote in his *Report*, "that certain nations grant bounties on the exportation of particular commodities, to enable their own workmen to undersell and supplant all competitors, in the countries to which those commodities are sent. Hence the undertakers of a new manufacture have to contend not only with the natural disadvantages of a new undertaking, but with the gratuities and remunerations which other governments bestow."

So, if America is to compete in a world where virtually every country is protecting its own trade and helping manufacturers in critical areas and technologies, only the government of the United States can overcome those structural challenges. "To be enabled to contend [against these foreign competitors] with success," he wrote, "it is evident, that the interference and aid of their own government are indispensable."

Manufacturing goods in America was also, Hamilton pointed out, absolutely essential to the nation's security militarily. "Not only the wealth," he wrote in his *Report*, "but the independence and security of a Country, appear to be materially connected with the prosperity of manufactures. Every nation, with a view to those great objects, ought to endeavor to possess within itself all the essentials of national supply. These comprise the means of *Subsistence habitation clothing and defence* [emphasis in the original]."

Hamilton drew from history the lesson that homegrown manufacturing, particularly of items necessary to normal life and a functioning army, was essential to national security as well as for national prosperity. "The possession of these [domestic manufacturers] is necessary to the perfection of the body politic, to the safety as well as to the welfare of the society . . . and in the various crises which await a state, it must severely feel the effects of any such deficiency."

You can run your own thought experiment to demonstrate Hamilton's perspective. Imagine that we got into a conflict with China and they simply shut off the flow of all goods manufactured there to the US. Walmart would empty in a week or two, as would most Amazon departments and other stores across the country. Commerce would grind to a halt, and a shock greater than the Republican Great Depression would set in, if outright war wasn't provoked.

So much for neoliberal trade policy helping ensure the security and prosperity of our nation.

CHAPTER 25

How China Escaped Neoliberalism

While America, Chile, Russia, Argentina, and a dozen other nations were experimenting with (and being devastated by) Milton Friedman's and Ronald Reagan's neoliberalism, China's Deng Xiaoping decided instead to adopt Alexander Hamilton's plan in full.[1]

I spent the month of November 1986 in China; it was then deeply impoverished, just beginning to recover from Mao's revolution and the famines it brought. In that decade, they rejected Friedman's advice and went with Hamilton.

The tallest building in Beijing, where I lived and studied, was a 10-story Hilton (as I recall) hotel. The city's air was thick with smoke from the millions of tiny coal fires that people used to heat a single room in their homes. Standing in Tiananmen Square I watched a river of black bicycles flow past every day on the major highway nearby. Every 10 minutes or so, a single black limousine would go by.

China was at a crossroads, and Deng Xiaoping knew it. The country had decided, in 1984 with the publication of the Communist Party's *Decision on the Economic System Reform*, that what they'd been doing since Mao definitely wasn't working.

Within China, economists who'd followed Friedman and his neoliberals encouraged the government to jump into "shock therapy" as Chile had done and Russia would soon do. Within China, they referred to this transition as "One Big Step."

Other Chinese economists, familiar with Hamilton's American Plan and how it had created prosperity for the US, were pushing a variation on it that involved a gradual transition from a government-run economy to a free enterprise one with strict regulation. These Hamiltonians and Keynesians referred to their proposal as "Groping for Stones to Cross the River."

For two years, these two factions fought it out until finally, in the summer of the year I was there, Deng and the Communist Party made their decision, announced on September 15, 1986. It fell to one of the country's top economists and advisers, Li Yining, to lay it out that day at Peking University in a speech titled "Comparing the Two Schools of Reform Thought."

As Isabella M. Weber, an assistant professor of economics at the University of Massachusetts Amherst, wrote in her brilliant book *How China Escaped Shock Therapy*, "[Premier] Zhao Ziyang ultimately gave up on [neoliberal] package reform. This plan had appeared like a comprehensive solution in theory, but it proved infeasible in practice. Zhao came around to arguing that the basic challenge of economic reform was enlivening enterprises. This, Zhao realized, could not be achieved in parallel with a radical price reform that endangered the stability of economy and society while bearing little prospect for success. The first, most shocking element of shock therapy, overnight price liberalization, was aborted."[2]

One of the main points of debate had been the Chinese concern about "morality." Weber noted that the neoliberal "reformers held that morality was to be replaced by free competition among individuals. . . . The ancient scholar officials held that markets were to be subordinate to the moral order of society. For the shock therapists, all realms of society were to be subordinate to a universal market."

China escaped embracing shock therapy—twice in two years—and ultimately signed on for the kind of economic revolution we had here in America between 1793 and 1980 instead of going down the path that Russia and others would tread.

Thus, today we can compare neoliberal policies in Russia against a Chinese variation on Hamilton's American Plan put into place in China.

Between 1990 and 2017, Russia's share of world GDP collapsed from 3.7 percent to a mere 2.2 percent, as the real income of the bottom 99 percent of Russians actually fell between those years. The result was both economic and social devastation, as Weber wrote: "As a result of shock therapy, Russia experienced a rise in mortality beyond that of any previous peacetime experiences of an industrialized country."[3]

China's working class, meanwhile, saw their income increase fourfold during the same period, and China's share of world GDP rose from a mere 2.2 percent to fully one-eighth of the entire planet's GDP.[4]

CHAPTER 26

America Adopted Neoliberalism, and All I Got Was This Made-in-China T-Shirt

But that was 1986 and this is now, after China's 35 years of using their version of Hamilton's American Plan. China's rejection of neoliberalism and adoption of Hamilton's plan transformed that nation into the world's second-richest in less than 30 years: it was the single-most-rapid positive transformation of any nation's economy in the history of the world.

To add insult to injury for an America stuck with Reagan's neoliberalism, when we buy Chinese goods, they get our dollars. Dollars that eventually must return to America in the form of what's called *direct foreign investment.* In other words, they're taking our money for the products they make and then buying our country with it. At the end of the day, dollars have to be redeemed in the US because they're created here.

Have you seen what housing prices are doing? Foreign purchases of US housing were over $11 billion and made up 4 percent of all home sales in 2020.[1] They have slowed down a bit recently: they totaled over $100 billion a year through most of the previous decade.[2] In just 2017 and 2018, Chinese buyers alone picked up more than 80,000 US residential properties.[3]

Foreign buyers now own 30 million acres of American farmland (an amount that has doubled in the past two decades).[4] Remember Smithfield Foods, the huge industrial meatpacking operation where President Trump ordered workers back to the slaughter lines even though there was a pandemic? The largest producer in America, they have more than 500 industrial-style animal operations, factory farms, and the company is Chinese owned.[5]

Fully 40 percent of the asset value of all companies in America is now foreign owned: that's the wealth of nations created by manufacturing outside America being used to buy our country piece-by-piece.[6] Chinese investors and the Chinese government also own over $1 trillion in US Treasuries, our national debt.[7]

We've moved so much manufacturing to China that we can't make much of anything—from missiles to cars to airplanes—without Chinese parts.

And this doesn't begin to touch the damage China could do to America if it were to decide, for example, that it would cut off *all* exports and begin to dump our Treasuries because we were defending Taiwan—an increasingly likely scenario. If you think we're having a crisis today, imagine if within two months every Chinese product were gone from every American store.

Reagan, Bush, and Clinton's implementation of Milton Friedman's neoliberal free trade agenda gutted the American middle class, sold off our companies and real estate to foreign interests, and in 2021 caused supply-chain disruptions that threatened any semblance of an economic recovery.

As a direct result of neoliberal trade policies, there's too much finished product coming into America and not enough leaving our factories for foreign shores: this is called our *trade deficit*. To quote NPR's *Planet Money* headline, it's "Too Much Import, Too Little Export."[8]

As noted in *Forbes*, "So, we send dollars abroad to pay for those things made by foreigners. Very few of them set fire to those dollars, they nearly all use them to do something with."[9] Ultimately, that something is to buy American infrastructure.

Our trade deficit in 2020 was over $610 billion and averaged around $700 billion a year in the lead-up to the Great Recession of 2008.[10] Eventually every one of those dollars will come back here in exchange for ownership of part of America going overseas.

In 1975, we had a $16 billion trade *surplus* ($81.5 billion in today's dollars).[11] We had a mere $13 billion trade deficit when Reagan came into office in 1981.[12] By his last year in office, 1988, the cumulative trade deficit for his presidency was $685 billion ($3.4 trillion in today's dollars).[13]

That deficit was offset by foreign entities' buying US real estate, US companies, US land, US securities, and US debt. It made a lot of already-morbidly rich asset-selling Americans a lot richer.

But what did it give average workers? Bubkes. Less than bubkes, actually: fewer than half of Americans are even *in* the middle class anymore.[14]

Donald Trump said many of these same things. In that, he was just echoing the message that nearly won Bernie Sanders the Democratic nomination for president in 2016 and keeps progressive Democrat Sherrod Brown comfortably ensconced in his Senate seat in otherwise-red Ohio.

Even though Americans can't explain the consequences of neoliberal trade policies, they understand the principle. When a country manufactures things, it creates wealth. When it shifts to a service economy, where people pay each other to feed or massage them, no wealth is created: it's simply moving money around.

While neoliberalism was brought to America by Reagan, Clinton jumped on the bandwagon too, so opposing it has been an uneasy task for both Republicans and Democrats for the past three decades. Hillary Clinton wouldn't acknowledge that Trump's willingness to challenge that neoliberal consensus and speak the truth (in his own confused way) had to account for much of his Electoral College margin of victory in 2016.

Nonetheless, even though most Americans don't know the gory details or history I've laid out here, they do know that we used to make things in America and it made us rich, and we no longer make much here (outside of guns and military weaponry) and it's making us poor.

It's so entrenched that *IndustryWeek* reported in October 2019, a year *before* the COVID-19 pandemic disrupted things, "Three years after Donald Trump campaigned for president pledging a factory renaissance, the opposite appears to be happening. Manufacturing made up 11% of gross domestic product in the second quarter, the smallest share in data going back to 1947 and down from 11.1% in the prior period, a Commerce Department report showed."[15]

Back in the day when neoliberals were leading the free trade charge with Tom Friedman's book *The Lexus and the Olive Tree: Understanding Globalization*, we at least had a robust discussion of its impact: today that's largely confined to the few remaining union halls.[16]

Ross Perot took almost one in five votes for president in 1992 because American voters were so horrified about the "giant sucking sound" from the south that he predicted would happen if neoliberal trade policies were expanded by signing the North American Free Trade Agreement, which the Bush administration had negotiated.

Perot, it turns out, was right. As were Henry VII, Alexander Hamilton, Franklin D. Roosevelt, Zhao Ziyang, and Deng Xiaoping.

Neoliberal Trade Policy Rejected by South Korea

A more contemporary example of the application of that wisdom can be seen in South Korea. In the 1960s, South Korea was an undeveloped nation whose major exports were human hair (for wigs), tungsten, and fish, and whose average annual income was around $400 per working family.

Today it's a major industrial power with an average annual per capita income of over $32,000, and it beats the United States in its rate of college attendance, exports, and life span. South Korea did it by following Hamilton's American Plan, closing its economy and promoting its export industries. A decade earlier, Japan had done the same thing. Forty years earlier, Germany had done it.

In July 2009, with no evident irony or understanding of how South Korea had gone about becoming a modern economic powerhouse, President Obama lectured the countries of Africa during his visit to Ghana. As the *New York Times* reported, "Mr. Obama said that when his father came to the United States, his home country of Kenya had an economy as large as that of South Korea per capita. Today, he noted, Kenya remains impoverished and politically unstable, while South Korea has become an economic powerhouse."[1]

In the same day's newspaper, the lead editorial, titled "Tangled Trade Talks," repeated the essence of the mantra of its confused op-ed writer Thomas L. Friedman, that so-called free trade was the solution to a nation's economic ills. "There are few things that could do more damage to the already battered global economy than an old-fashioned trade war," the *Times* opined. "So we have been increasingly worried by the protectionist rhetoric and policies being espoused by politicians across the globe and in this country."[2]

But South Korea did not ride the free trade train to success.

South Korean economist Ha-Joon Chang details South Korea's economic ascent in his 2008 book *Bad Samaritans: The Myth of Free Trade and the Secret History of Capitalism*.[3]

In 1961, South Korea was as poor as Kenya, with an $82 per capita annual income and many obstacles to economic strength. The country's main exports were primary commodities such as the aforementioned tungsten, fish, and human hair for wigs.

That's how the Korean technology giant Samsung started—by exporting fish, fruits, and vegetables. Today, it's one of the world's largest conglomerates by revenue. By throwing out "free trade" and embracing "protectionism" during the 1960s, South Korea managed to do in 50 years what it took the United States 100 years and Britain 150 years to do.

After a military coup in 1961, Gen. Park Chung-hee implemented short-term plans for South Korea's economic development. He instituted the Heavy and Chemical Industrialization program, and South Korea's first steel mill and modern shipyard went into production. In addition, South Korea began producing its own cars and used import tariffs to discourage imports.

Electronics, machinery, and chemical plants soon followed, all sponsored or subsidized and tariff-protected by the government. Between 1972 and 1979, the per capita income grew over five times. In addition, new protectionist slogans were adopted by South Korean citizens. For example, it was viewed as civic duty to publicly shame anyone caught smoking foreign cigarettes.

All money made from exports went into developing industry. South Korea enacted import bans, high tariffs, and excise taxes on thousands of products.

In the 1980s, South Korea was still far from the industrialized West, but it had built a solid middle class. South Korea's transformation was, to quote Chang, as if "Haiti had turned into Switzerland." This transformation was accomplished through protecting fledgling industries with high tariffs and subsidies and only gradually opening the country to global competition.

In addition, the government ran or heavily funded many of the larger industries, at least until they were globally competitive. It ran or regulated the banks and therefore the credit. It controlled foreign exchange and used its currency reserves to import machinery and industrial imports.

At the same time, the government tightly controlled foreign investment in South Korea and largely ignored enforcement of foreign patent laws. It focused on exporting basic goods to fuel and protect its high-tech industries with tariffs and subsidies.

Had South Korea adopted the free trade policies espoused by neoliberals, it would still be exporting fish.

Another favorite free trade example is the success of Toyota's Lexus luxury car, immortalized in Thomas Friedman's book *The Lexus and the Olive Tree*. But again, the reality is quite different from what Friedman naively portrays in his book. In fact, Japan subsidized Toyota not only in its development but even after it failed terribly in the American markets in the late 1950s.

In addition, early in Toyota's development, Japan kicked out foreign competitors like GM. Thus, because the Japanese government financed Toyota at a loss for roughly 20 years, built high tariff and other barriers to competitive imports, and initially subsidized exports, auto manufacturing was able to get a strong foothold, and we now think of Japanese exports as being synonymous with automobiles.

CHAPTER 28

Reverse Privatization of Core Government Functions

During World War II, my dad told me, the Army had cooks, laundry workers, radio stations for entertainment and news, truck drivers, and its own security forces. The benefit of having soldiers doing all these things, he said, was that if their base was attacked by the Germans or the Japanese, every cook, laundry person, truck driver, DJ, and Army cop could simply pick up their own rifle and join the fray.

When neoliberalism came to our military in the 1980s, tens of thousands of jobs were taken from our service members in uniform and given instead to private, for-profit "military contractors." Thus, for 20 years or so in Iraq and Afghanistan, we had private contractor truck drivers (among hundreds of other jobs), some earning more than $100,000 a year,[1] as well as locals who provided cooking and other services for the US military in Bosnia in the 1990s;[2] and when a base was attacked, the low-paid soldiers had to not only fight the enemy but also provide security for the contractor cooks and drivers.[3]

In 2019, there were roughly 35,000 US troops in the Iraq and Afghanistan theaters of the Middle East, each paid a simple government salary. There were also that year 53,000 private contractors, each typically paid three or more times what soldiers made, and the companies that sent them also marked up those payments to account for support and profits.[4]

As Heidi Peltier of the Watson Institute at Brown University noted for their "Costs of War" research project: "In 2019, the Pentagon spent $370 billion on contracting—more than half the total defense budget of $676 billion and a whopping 164% higher than its spending on contractors in 2001."[5]

Peltier wrote that this began formally within the Pentagon in 1983 and laid it at the feet of neoliberalism:

The 1980s brought a wave of privatization of public services, part of the larger movement sometimes referred to as neoliberalism. "Chicago-school" economics, which in the 1970s and 1980s became an increasingly influential school of thought led by Milton Friedman and George Stigler (economists at the University of Chicago), proposed that free markets were superior to government planning and that the government impeded markets and should be deregulated and privatized as much as possible. Conservative think tanks, such as the Heritage Foundation, pushed the idea that private providers would necessarily be more cost-efficient than government due to the nature of competition. According to this neoliberal economic theory, competitive pressures would drive down costs and increase quality, leading to both cheaper and better products and services than the government could produce itself.[6]

This began in a huge way during the Reagan administration, when Stephen Moore wrote triumphantly for the Heritage Foundation in 1986, "Privatization has come of age. The Reagan Administration's FY 1987 budget argues that considerable budget savings can be achieved without cutting services but by transferring government functions to the private sector—in short, by privatization. . . . The Reagan administration has been committed to contracting out commercial services since 1981."[7]

What started as an experiment with Reagan's military budget has become simply the way things are now done. It was stupid and inefficient from the start, but also insanely profitable for the private military contractors, who turned the zip codes around Washington, DC, where their CEOs lived into the most expensive in America, blowing away Beverly Hills and New York. And as long as defense contractors kept sending their "free speech" dollars to American politicians, those politicians kept putting private contractors into everything they could.

As Edward Snowden revealed, more than half of our intelligence services have now been outsourced to private companies, too.[8] It's a boondoggle, but at least it's "free" of government interference or regulation: just keep writing the checks. And work done by private contractors isn't subject to the same congressional or public scrutiny that government transparency laws require of most federal agencies: it's a great place to bury sleazy payoffs, torture, and even illegal spying on American citizens.

The same thing has happened across America as formerly publicly owned utilities (power, water, sewage) have been privatized into corporate hands and then turned from public services into cash machines for investors.

Breaking neoliberalism means reversing all of these policies that have harmed average Americans while making a handful of investors fabulously rich.

CHAPTER 29

Break Up the Monopolies

Neoliberals don't consider monopolies to be a problem because having government decide "how big is too big" would be a breach of the free market.

But here in the real world, monopolies are a real problem, costing average Americans a small fortune while preventing entrepreneurs from jumping into the marketplace with new and innovative ideas.

Breaking up monopolies and oligopolies in virtually every industry in America is an essential part of reversing the damage that neoliberalism has done to the American economy and our middle class.

CHAPTER 30

Progressive Populism to Replace Progressive Neoliberalism

America's big neoliberal experiment began in earnest when President Reagan explicitly and openly abandoned the populist and Keynesian system that FDR had put together in the 1930s to get us out of the Republican Great Depression. Reagan advanced a conservative form of neoliberalism that packaged free trade, financialization of the economy, and destruction of labor unions with the white populism that Nixon had pioneered with his Southern Strategy.

White men might be losing their good-paying jobs to Mexico and Asia, but they could be assured that Reagan and the GOP would do everything they could to maintain the systems of white privilege while suppressing the Black vote. Since the majority of white voters weren't losing or downscaling their jobs, they threw in with Reagan and the Old South.

The backlash to Reagan's economic and trade policies was slow to form (it's taken 40 years, really), but the reaction to his naked racism and war against affirmative action animated the Democratic Party's base enough to bring Bill Clinton into the White House in 1992.

Clinton won fully 75 percent of the Black vote in the 1992 Super Tuesday primary, prompting the *New York Times* and

NPR to note that his candidacy "gives healthy evidence, probably for the first time since Robert Kennedy's Indiana primary campaign in 1968, that it is politically possible to bring poor blacks and blue-collar white voters together."[1]

Clinton reinvented American neoliberalism from Reagan's socially conservative and racist roots to be more inclusive of minorities and women, getting himself reelected on those issues even as the nation began hemorrhaging good-paying manufacturing jobs with a vengeance.

George W. Bush and Barack Obama continued the process of pushing neoliberalism, in its conservative and then progressive forms; neither challenged the core tenets of neoliberalism at all.

Obama put a friendlier face on it with his Obamacare legislation, but it was still giant insurance corporations that were calling all the shots, and Medicare was still forced to pay Big Pharma full retail for the same drugs on which the Veterans Administration was negotiating huge bulk discounts.

But by the end of Obama's presidency, Americans were wising up to what Reagan had wrought and wanted an alternative to both conservative *and* progressive neoliberalism.

That alternative, history shows, has always been populism, the politics of actually giving the people—the populace—what they want, rather than the neoliberal strategy of telling them that the market knows best what they need.

Two major populist forces came out of the 2015–2016 primaries: Donald Trump's conservative populism and Bernie Sanders's progressive populism.

Sanders's progressive populism exploded across the American landscape, drawing tens of thousands of people to rallies even in rural and small-town parts of the country. In those states like West Virginia where there were so few votes that the Democratic Party didn't intervene, Sanders steamrolled Hillary Clinton in the primary—for example, he carried every one of West Virginia's counties, beating Clinton by 15 points statewide.[2]

Neoliberals within both the Democratic Party and the media put their thumbs heavily on the scale for Hillary Clinton, who ran on a progressive neoliberal platform. The main thrust of her campaign, it seemed to many Democrats, was that it was high time for a woman to become president of the United States. Everything else was a slightly more progressive version of Bill Clinton's neoliberalism.

On the Republican side, the GOP itself was emasculated by Trump, and the national media put their thumb heavily on the Trump side, knowing that the showman would increase their ratings and thus their profits. The former NBC *Apprentice* reality-show star got so much coverage during the 2015–2016 primaries that then-CEO of CBS News Les Moonves told an investor call, "I've never seen anything like this, and this is going to be a very good year for us. Sorry. It's a terrible thing to say. But, bring it on, Donald. Keep going. . . . It may not be good for America, but it's damn good for CBS."[3]

As Emily Stewart wrote about Trump and the media for *The Street*: "The real estate magnate got $4.96 billion in free earned media in the year leading up to the presidential election, according to data from tracking firm mediaQuant. He received $5.6 billion [in free media] throughout the entirety of his campaign, more than Hillary Clinton, Bernie Sanders, Ted Cruz, Paul Ryan and Marco Rubio combined."[4]

Populism sells, although America's corporate media would rather have conservative neoliberalism (which keeps profits high and taxes low) than progressive neoliberalism (which would raise their taxes and increase some regulation).

And with a progressive neoliberal running against a conservative populist (with a little help from Russian oligarchs and Facebook), the populist ended up in the White House.

At least it *seemed* that a populist had won the Electoral College. In fact, Trump governed in a way that *seemed* populist, with daily press hits and lots of rallies, but in fact he simply continued Reagan's and Bush's conservative neoliberal agendas.

He didn't do a thing to rein in Wall Street or rebuild America's infrastructure (which neoliberal policies had left with a $4 trillion hole), he gave a massive tax break to himself and the nation's wealthiest people, and he engaged in massive and illegal self-dealing and theft from the government and thus the public.

His supporters thought they were getting populism, but it was all talk: Trump continued Reagan's conservative neoliberalism with a few symbolic tariffs on Chinese goods thrown in to maintain the illusion.

Within four years, Republican voters had figured out Trump's scam so completely that in the election of 2020, he not only lost the Electoral College but lost the popular vote by around seven million.

Joe Biden came into office in January 2021 and, being a smart and experienced politician, realized that the winds had shifted away from neoliberalism. He immediately began to undo some of Trump's deregulatory policies, but when he tried to reverse the Trump tax cuts, he got hit hard by opposition from Democratic neoliberals in both the House and the Senate.

The big lesson of all this is that the era of neoliberalism—both progressive and conservative—is drawing to a close in America. The experiment has been tried and failed, leaving millions broke and homeless in its wake.

The magical invisible hand of the free market was just that of the financial industry playing puppet master; markets must be regulated to work fairly, and manufacturing must be domestic to protect and advance the interests of the nation.

Populism—either in its conservative form, as played out in Russia and Hungary, or in its progressive form, as played out in Scandinavia—is the new coin of the political realm.

Republicans have already figured this out: Trump pushed it right into their faces in the 2016 primaries, and Republicans are already falling over each other to demonstrate who's the firmest against teaching America's racial history and who can bring our factories back from China.

Democrats are slower off the block: Bernie Sanders and his compatriots never shattered the Democratic Party the way Trump did the GOP, and there's still a river of cash flowing from corporate America into the pockets of neoliberal Democratic politicians.

The direction of the Democratic Party will be known by January 2025, and if it continues to cling to neoliberalism, the party will endure a crisis like it hasn't seen since the election of 1920.

On the other hand, if Democrats embrace the Bernie Sanders/Elizabeth Warren type of progressive populism that

FDR used to end the Republican Great Depression, they may control American politics for several generations, like FDR's Democratic Party did from 1933 to 1981.

CHAPTER 31

Standing
on the Edge

Do we stand on the edge of a grand new progressive era, with good wages for all, racial and gender equality and justice, and a reduction of the political power of reactionary forces in America? Or will the next president gleefully overthrow American democracy, shutter the free press, and imprison those who object?

When Mussolini put Antonio Gramsci, the founder of Italy's Communist Party, in prison in 1927, Gramsci wrote from his prison cell that "the old is dying and the new cannot be born; in this interregnum a great variety of morbid symptoms appear."[1]

Two forces in American politics are similarly on a collision course today: neoliberalism and progressivism. In the friction zone between the two, the "morbid symptom" of Trump's white-power neofascism is claiming territory and has largely seized the power structures of the GOP.

Whether American history goes in cycles, as William Strauss and Neil Howe suggest in *The Fourth Turning*, or merely "rhymes," as in the apocryphal quote from Mark Twain, we *can* identify periods when a particular political and economic philosophy holds court—and the periods when philosophies or regimes begin to collapse.[2]

The Fourth Turning posits roughly 80-year cycles in American history, each ending with an economic crash and a war, then each rebooting into a new progressive era: the Depression of the early 1770s and the American Revolution, the Panic of 1856 and the Civil War, the 1930s Republican Great Depression and World War II.

It's been about 80 years since the end of that war—indicating, if this theory is right, that a crash and war may be around the corner.

Another way of looking at the cycles of American history is through the lens of "regimes," as articulated by Stephen Skowronek in his 1997 book *The Politics Presidents Make*[3] and revived in a *New York Times* op-ed in 2021 by Corey Robin. "The Jeffersonian regime lasted from 1800 to 1828," Robin wrote, "the Jacksonian regime, from 1828 to 1860; the Republican regime, from 1860 to 1932; the New Deal order, from 1932 to 1980."[4]

The Reagan order is thus now almost certainly in its calcification stage, becoming brittle, more fragile, and less vigorous as inevitably happens with every turn of regimes.

In my opinion, the progressive movement—for example, the unionization effort where Kellogg's fired their workers and irate young people crashed their job-application server—is the ascendant group that will soon take power and hold the country for another turn of history.

Evidence abounds that the Reagan era or regime is rapidly disintegrating; that the Trump neofascist movement isn't strong or broad-based enough to replace it (although they can cause considerable violence and distress); and, as in the

1930s and 1960s, that a young progressive movement is rapidly acquiring and consolidating political power.

If I'm right and that's what's happening, it's almost certainly because Americans are realizing that Reagan's neoliberalism regime (which was carried on by the following five presidents) was largely a scam designed to disempower the working class while enriching the already well-off.

All of its vaunted rhetoric about fiscal responsibility and conservative values was just a smokescreen to hide naked theft, racism, and misogyny.

In overthrowing FDR's New Deal politics and economics, Reagan's era destroyed most of the American labor movement, shifted trillions in both income and wealth from the middle class to the top 1 percent, consolidated business and the wealth it creates into the hands of monopolies in every sector of our economy, and moved over 60,000 factories and tens of millions of good-paying jobs to low-wage countries, all while fattening the money bins of the morbidly rich with the Reagan, Bush, and Trump tax cuts.

But nothing stays the same. Circumstances change, failures are exposed, new generations acquire power as old generations pass away. If there's a constant to politics, it is this: every new cycle is eventually rejected and replaced as time moves forward.

Gramsci wondered, "Will the interregnum, the crisis whose historically normal solution is blocked in this way, necessarily be resolved in favour of a restoration of the old?" Or, would this "lead in the long run to widespread skepticism and a new 'arrangement'"?[5]

After all, Gramsci noted, that "new arrangement" would require "a reduction of the highest superstructures" of politics and society, "in other words, the possibility and necessity of creating a new culture."

Bifurcation, a splitting apart, appears to be the current state of America, but significant social change always happens just as opposite forces like these battle for the approval of the larger culture and its media, to soon be followed by its voters.

Corey Robin points out in his *New York Times* piece how "regimes grow brittle," and, much as the Reagan regime replaced FDR's New Deal regime, we may be at the end of our generation's 40-year neoliberal experiment (my phrase, not his).[6]

For this to actually happen, though, it's going to take not just a cultural shift but an actual change in the political and legal structures that Reagan's neoliberalism and its reactionary predecessors erected.

The question is, can the forces arrayed against such change, from corporate media (and social media) to packed courts to cranky billionaires, be overcome?

In a brilliant little (63-page) book, *The Old Is Dying and the New Cannot Be Born*, whose title came from Gramsci's famous quote, Nancy Fraser argues that progressive populism is today on the verge of replacing neoliberalism in its several forms.[7]

She makes a strong argument, although she says candidly that it will take all of us, particularly requiring a widespread mobilization of the young people, if we are to succeed. They are the ones who will face the worst outcomes, from the ravages of climate change to the rise of neofascist bullies, if we fail.

The neoliberal era is over, and the next few elections will determine what type of populism rules America. Will we become, as we emerge from the wreckage of four decades of neoliberalism, an American version of neoliberal Russia or of Democratic Socialist Denmark? Or will we invent our own new way, hopefully one that can once again lead the world?

Only time will tell. But we can all pitch in to bring about a new and better America. Tag, you're it!

NOTES

Foreword

1. Thomas Friedman, *The Lexus and the Olive Tree: Understanding Globalization* (New York: Picador, 2000), 104.

Introduction

1. https://www.theguardian.com/books/2016/apr/15/neoliberalism -ideology-problem-george-monbiot
2. https://en.wikipedia.org/wiki/Chamber_of_Fasces_and_Corporations

Chapter 1. Save Us from the Utopians

1. https://plato.stanford.edu/entries/plato-utopia/
2. https://theopenutopia.org/full-text/book-ii-of-utopia/
3. Karl Popper, *The Open Society and Its Enemies* (Princeton, NJ: Princeton University Press, 1994).
4. "We have set ourselves only one aim: the people. All paths upon which we set our feet will lead to this purpose. Furthermore, we recognize that unless one wants to destroy everything, one must start and proceed on this path with many compromises and many leniencies. But the movement is not the temporary appearance of one man. Many years ago, in *Mein Kampf* I said that National Socialism will put its stamp on the next thousand years of Germany history. You cannot conceive it without National Socialism." From Adolf Hitler's January 30, 1941, speech at the Berlin Sports Palace.
5. I tell more of this story in my book *ADHD: Hunter in a Farmer's World*, for which Will wrote a kind blurb. He's since passed away.
6. https://factsanddetails.com/southeast-asia/Cambodia/sub5_2b /entry-2852.html
7. https://www.rbth.com/longreads/1917-bolshevik-revolution/
8. David P. Jordan, *The Revolutionary Career of Maximilien Robespierre* (Chicago, IL: University of Chicago Press, 1985), 2.
9. Robert B. Reich, *The System: Who Rigged It, How We Fix It* (New York: Alfred A. Knopf, 2020).
10. Reich, *The System.*
11. Reich.

Chapter 2. The Birth of Neoliberalism

1. https://historyguild.org/the-bantu-expansion-how-bantu-people-changed -sub-saharan-africa/
2. Friedrich A. Hayek, *Law, Legislation and Liberty*, Vol. 2: *The Mirage of Social Justice* (Chicago, IL: University of Chicago Press, 1976).
3. The Mont Pelerin Society, https://www.montpelerin.org/about-mps/.

4. Kim Phillips-Fein, *Invisible Hands: The Businessmen's Crusade Against the New Deal* (New York: W. W. Norton & Co., 2010).

5. https://www.montpelerin.org/statement-of-aims/

6. Ibid.

7. President Abraham Lincoln, First Annual Message to Congress, December 3, 1861 (the "State of the Union"), https://www.presidency.ucsb.edu /documents/first-annual-message-9.

8. This was on my radio program about a decade ago, and while I can't find the exact date of the conversation, I'm quite sure that Moore wouldn't deny it: he's proud of his position that capitalism is a necessary precondition for democracy and thus superior to it.

Chapter 3. Neoliberalism's Fathers: Mises, Hayek, and Friedman

1. Lord Acton, "Review of Sir Erskine May's *Democracy in Europe*," 1878, quoted by F. A. Hayek in *The Road to Serfdom*, ed. Bruce Caldwell (Chicago, IL: University of Chicago Press, 2007, reprint ed.).

2. Ludwig von Mises, *Human Action: A Treatise on Economics* (Irvington-on-Hudson, NY: Foundation for Economic Education, 1998, orig. pub. 1949).

3. Ludwig von Mises, *Liberalism: In the Classical Tradition*, https://mises.org /library/liberalism-classical-tradition/html/p/29.

4. Ibid.

5. Ludwig von Mises, *Socialism: An Economic and Sociological Analysis*, trans. J. Kahane (Eastford, CT: Martino Fine Books, 2012, reprint of 1962 ed.), 498.

6. Ibid.

7. Ibid.

8. Mises, *Human Action*, chapter 24, https://www.econlib.org/library/Mises /HmA/msHmA.html?chapter_num=27#book-reader.

9. Hayek, *Law, Legislation and Liberty*, Vol. 2: *The Mirage of Social Justice*, 189.

10. Mises, *Socialism*, 498.

11. I detail this at length, with quotes from Otto von Bismark, in *The Hidden History of American Healthcare*.

12. https://www.bbc.co.uk/bitesize/guides/z9y64j6/revision/8

13. F. A. Hayek, *The Road to Serfdom*, ed. Bruce Caldwell (Chicago, IL: University of Chicago Press, 2007, reprint ed.).

14. https://onlinelibrary.wiley.com/doi/abs/10.1111/j.1468-0289.2009.00473.x

15. Hayek, *The Road to Serfdom*.

16. Ibid.

17. Rand Paul, *The Case Against Socialism* (New York: Broadside Books, 2019).

18. George Sylvester Viereck, "1923 Interview with Adolf Hitler," *American Monthly*, in Famous Trials, https://famous-trials.com/hitler/2529-1923 -interview-with-adolf-hitler.

19. https://encyclopedia.ushmm.org/content/en/article/the-enabling-act
20. Hayek, *The Road to Serfdom*.
21. Ibid.
22. Milton and Rose Friedman, *Two Lucky People: Memoirs* (Chicago, IL: University of Chicago Press, 1998).
23. https://www.reaganfoundation.org/ronald-reagan/reagan-quotes -speeches/inaugural-address-2/
24. https://www.ushistory.org/documents/ask-not.htm
25. Milton Friedman, *Capitalism and Freedom*, 40th Anniversary Ed. (Chicago, IL: University of Chicago Press, 2002), 1.
26. https://www.bbc.com/news/uk-politics-38553797
27. From the US Declaration of Independence, 1776.
28. Friedman, *Capitalism and Freedom*, 149.
29. Mark Ames, "When Congress Busted Milton Friedman (and Libertarianism Was Created by Big Business Lobbyists)," November 16, 2012, NSFW Corp., https://web.archive.org/web/20201124114335/https://www .nsfwcorp.com/dispatch/milton-friedman/.
30. Ibid.
31. https://admin.fee.org/files/docLib/Roofs-or-Ceilings.pdf
32. https://www.nytimes.com/1970/09/13/archives/a-friedman-doctrine -the-social-responsibility-of-business-is-to.html
33. Naomi Klein, *The Shock Doctrine: The Rise of Disaster Capitalism* (New York: Picador, 2007).

Chapter 4. Neoliberalism Goes to Work

1. Letter to Albert Gallatin, December 13, 1803.

Chapter 5. Worldwide Neoliberalism Experiments

1. https://unctad.org/system/files/official-document/gds20091_en.pdf

Chapter 6. Milton Friedman Hearts General Pinochet

1. C. J. Tesar and Sheila C. Tesar, "Recent Chilean Copper Policy," *Geography* 58, no. 1 (1973): 9–12, http://www.jstor.org/stable/40567857; Alan Angell, "Allende's First Year in Chile," *Current History* 62, no. 366 (1972): 76–80, http://www.jstor.org/stable/45312617.
2. Tesar and Tesar, "Recent Chilean Copper Policy."
3. Angell, "Allende's First Year in Chile."
4. https://www.nytimes.com/1972/07/03/archives/papers-show-itt-urged -us-to-help-oust-allende-suggestions-for.html
5. https://www.history.com/this-day-in-history/allende-dies-in-coup
6. https://www.thenation.com/article/archive/true-verdict-allende/

7. https://www.upi.com/Archives/1983/06/26/Chilean-protests-evoke
-memories-of-1973-coup/3585425448000/

8. https://www.independent.co.uk/news/world/americas/the-general
-willing-to-kill-his-people-to-win-the-battle-against-communism-427950
.html

9. https://www.nytimes.com/2006/12/11/world/americas/augusto
-pinochet-dictator-who-ruled-by-terror-in-chile-dies.html

10. Andre Gunder Frank, "Economic Genocide in Chile: Open Letter to Milton
Friedman and Arnold Harberger," *Economic and Political Weekly* 11, no. 24
(1976): 880–88, http://www.jstor.org/stable/4364704.

11. Friedman, *Two Lucky People.*

12. Klein, *The Shock Doctrine.*

13. https://www.nytimes.com/2006/12/11/world/americas/augusto
-pinochet-dictator-who-ruled-by-terror-in-chile-dies.html

14. https://promarket.org/2019/11/04/chiles-fall-from-grace-shows-the
-failures-of-neoliberalism/

15. Peter Kornbluh, *The Pinochet File: A Declassified Dossier on Atrocity and
Accountability* (New York: The New Press, 2003), 424.

Chapter 7. Neoliberalism Comes to America

1. https://money.cnn.com/2011/05/12/news/companies/walmart_selling
_american_products_2/index.htm

2. https://history.state.gov/milestones/1969-1976/nixon-shock

3. Ibid.

4. https://history.state.gov/milestones/1969-1976/oil-embargo

5. Ibid.

6. https://millercenter.org/president/ford

7. https://millercenter.org/president/gerald-ford/key-events

8. https://www.thebalance.com/u-s-inflation-rate-history-by-year-and
-forecast-3306093

9. https://www.desmog.com/institute-economic-affairs/

10. https://www.nytimes.com/1982/02/11/business/reagan-terms-inflation
-fight-critical-priority.html

11. https://www.nytimes.com/1991/11/28/business/congress-votes-100
-billion-bank-and-s-l-aid.html

12. https://www.newsweek.com/anne-gorsuch-new-bill-abolish-epa-551382

13. https://www.washingtonpost.com/archive/politics/1981/06/30/the-watt
-controversy/d591699b-3bc2-46d2-9059-fb5d2513c3da/?itid=lk_inline
_manual_10

14. https://abcnews.go.com/WNT/Politics/story?id=1171385&page=1

15. https://www.dol.gov/general/aboutdol/history/dolorigabridge

16. https://www.washingtonpost.com/local/obituaries/raymond-donovan
    -dead/2021/06/05/2f61a3a6-1c97-11e8-b2d9-08e748f892c0_story.html
17. https://www.epi.org/publication/ceo-compensation-2018/
18. https://usafacts.org/articles/labor-union-membership/

Chapter 8. Bill Clinton Hearts the Neoliberal Revolution

1. https://www.nytimes.com/2019/07/09/business/economy/ross-perot
   -nafta-trade.html
2. Ibid.
3. https://www.cbsnews.com/news/some-us-military-parts-imported-from
   -china/
4. I do a deep dive on this in *The Hidden History of Monopolies*.
5. Al From, *The New Democrats and the Return to Power* (New York: St. Martin's
   Press, 2013).
6. https://www.nytimes.com/1996/12/08/opinion/foreign-affairs-big-mac-i
   .html
7. Lawrence R. Klein and Marshall Pomer, eds., *The New Russia: Transition
   Gone Awry* (Stanford, CA: Stanford University Press, 2001); Vladimir Mau,
   Russian Economic Reforms as Seen by an Insider: Success or Failure? (London,
   UK: Royal Institute of International Affairs, 2000).
8. Klein, *The Shock Doctrine*.
9. https://www.pbs.org/weta/washingtonweek/web-video/era-big
   -government-over-clintons-1996-state-union
10. https://kenan.ethics.duke.edu/wp-content/uploads/2018/01/Moodys
    _Text20151.pdf

Chapter 9. George W. Bush Pushes Neoliberalism Even Further

1. https://www.motherjones.com/politics/2011/09/great-gop-medicare-lie/
2. https://www.forbes.com/sites/douggollan/2017/09/22/a-look-inside-the
   -private-jets-of-trump-administration-insiders/?sh=4bcbbcfa5168
3. https://abcnews.go.com/Business/Politics/story?id=8140184
4. https://www.sourcewatch.org/index.php/Project_for_the_New
   _American_Century
5. https://www.theguardian.com/world/2002/aug/11/iraq.oil
6. https://www.amazon.com/Charge-Keep-Journey-White-House/dp
   /0060957921/
7. https://russbaker.com/archives/Guerrilla%20News%20Network%20-%20
   Bush.htm
8. https://www.cnn.com/2003/US/04/11/sprj.irq.pentagon/
9. https://govinfo.library.unt.edu/cpa-iraq/regulations/20030919
   _CPAORD_37_Tax_Strategy_for_2003.pdf

10. https://www.unrefugees.org/emergencies/iraq/
11. https://www.iraqbodycount.org

Chapter 10. Neoliberalism Blows Up in Bush's Face

1. https://time.com/3956351/jack-bogle-index-fund/
2. https://www.washingtonpost.com/politics/spin-deride-attack-how
   -trumps-handling-of-trump-university-presaged-his-presidency
   /2020/07/24/7d3a327a-bfb8-11ea-9fdd-b7ac6b051dc8_story.html
3. https://truthout.org/articles/the-indisputable-role-of-credit-ratings
   -agencies-in-the-2008-collapse-and-why-nothing-has-changed/
4. https://www.thebalance.com/2008-financial-crisis-timeline-3305540
5. https://thebasispoint.com/size-of-u-s-housing-market/
6. https://www.investopedia.com/articles/economics/09/subprime
   -market-2008.asp
7. https://www.thebalance.com/2008-financial-crisis-timeline-3305540

Chapter 11. Obama Rescues Neoliberalism from Itself

1. https://www.counterpunch.org/2009/10/16/barney-frank-the-bankers
   -consort/

Chapter 12. Trump Attacks Neoliberalism

1. https://www.taxpolicycenter.org/publications/analysis-donald-trumps
   -revised-tax-plan

Chapter 13. Biden Challenges Neoliberalism's Core Concepts

1. https://shero.substack.com/p/where-we-stand-on-build-back-better

Chapter 14. How Neoliberalism Changed America in 40 Years

1. https://truthout.org/articles/the-violence-of-organized-forgetting/
2. Herbert Spencer, *The Principles of Sociology*, 3 Vols. (New York: D. Appleton and Co., 3rd rev. ed., 1898), Vol. 2, Ch. XVIII, "The Industrial Type of Society" (1882), http://oll.libertyfund.org/titles/2632#lf1650-02_label_301.
3. https://archive.nytimes.com/www.nytimes.com/library/world/asia/052500clinton-trade-text.html
4. Faisal Islam, "How the West invited China to eat its lunch," *BBC News*, December 10, 2021, https://www.bbc.com/news/business-59610019.
5. https://www.costaricaexplorations.org/costa-rica-education-system/
6. https://robertreich.org/post/667491205931745280
7. https://www.cnbc.com/2021/06/11/how-hedge-funds-took-over-americas-struggling-newspaper-industry-.html

Chapter 15. Privatizing the Commons

1. https://www.professorbuzzkill.com/franklin-republic/
2. http://www.benjamin-franklin-history.org/lending-library/
3. Benjamin Franklin, *The Autobiography and Other Writings*, introduction by Jill Lepore (New York: Alfred A. Knopf/Everyman's Library, reprint ed., 2015).
4. https://truthout.org/articles/public-private-partnerships-are-quietly-hollowing-out-our-public-libraries/
5. https://www.volckeralliance.org/resources/true-size-government-1
6. https://www.inthepublicinterest.org/race-to-the-bottom-how-outsourcing-public-services-rewards-corporations-and-punishes-the-middle-class-2/
7. https://www.nytimes.com/2013/12/15/us/when-private-firms-run-schools-financial-secrecy-is-allowed.html?searchResultPosition=1
8. Ibid.
9. https://www.researchgate.net/publication/272744049_Overlooking_Oversight_A_Lack_of_Oversight_in_the_Garden_State_Is_Placing_New_Jersey_Residents_and_Assets_at_Risk
10. https://www.inthepublicinterest.org/wp-content/uploads/contracts.broaderimpacts.greenwood.march-2014.REVISED-AND-FINAL-2.pdf
11. https://www.portman.senate.gov/newsroom/press-releases/portman-manchin-announce-value-money-analysis-bill-included-bipartisan
12. https://reason.org/wp-content/uploads/files/c2bbfe415eccfdff424a2bf7c8a20585.pdf
13. https://truthout.org/articles/public-private-partnerships-are-quietly-hollowing-out-our-public-libraries/
14. Ibid.

Chapter 17. Breaking with 40 Years of Neoliberalism

1. As quoted in Theodore S. Hamerow, *Reflections on History and Historians* (Madison, WI: University of Wisconsin Press, 1987), 220.

Chapter 18. #TaxTheRich

1. https://www.npr.org/sections/thetwo-way/2015/12/09/459087477/the-tipping-point-most-americans-no-longer-are-middle-class
2. https://www.bloomberg.com/news/articles/2021-10-08/top-1-earners-hold-more-wealth-than-the-u-s-middle-class

Chapter 19. Rebuilding a Middle Class Gutted by Neoliberalism

1. Thom Hartmann, *The Hidden History of Monopolies: How Big Business Destroyed the American Dream* (Oakland, CA: Berrett-Koehler Publishers, 2020).

2. https://www.payscale.com/research/US/Employer=Walmart.com/Hourly_Rate
3. Thomas Piketty, *Capital in the Twenty-First Century*, trans. Arthur Goldhammer (Cambridge, MA: The Belknap Press of Harvard University Press, 2017).

Chapter 20. Trade: Returning to Alexander Hamilton's American Plan

1. https://founders.archives.gov/documents/Hamilton/01-10-02-0001-0007
2. Adam Smith, *The Wealth of Nations*, ed. Edwin Cannan (New York: Bantam Classic, 2003), 572); also https://archive.org/stream/WealthOfNationsAdamSmith/Wealth%20of%20Nations_Adam%20Smith_djvu.txt "An Inquiry in to the Nature and Causes of the Wealth of Nations" Adam Smith, 1776.
3. Benson J. Lossing, "George Washington's Inauguration," from *Our Country*, vol. 2 (1877), http://www.publicbookshelf.com/public_html/Our_Country_vol_2/georgewas_bfb.html.
4. Rosemary E. Bachelor, *Washington's American Made Inaugural Clothes*, Suite 101, https://founders.archives.gov/documents/Washington /05-01-02-0197.

Chapter 21. What Is Real Wealth?

1. https://founders.archives.gov/documents/Hamilton/01-10-02-0001-0007

Chapter 22. Hamilton's 11-Step Plan Worked for 188 Years

1. https://founders.archives.gov/documents/Hamilton/01-10-02-0001-0007
2. Ibid.

Chapter 23. Tariffs Built America

1. https://www.huffpost.com/entry/billionaire-scion-tom-fri_b_26164
2. https://www.cfr.org/backgrounder/us-trade-deficit-how-much-does-it-matter

Chapter 24. But What About the Cost of American-Made Goods?

1. https://founders.archives.gov/documents/Hamilton/01-10-02-0001-0007

Chapter 25. How China Escaped Neoliberalism

1. Isabella M. Weber, *How China Escaped Shock Therapy: The Market Reform Debate* (New York: Routledge, 2021).
2. Weber, *How China Escaped Shock Therapy*.
3. Weber.
4. Weber.

Chapter 26. America Adopted Neoliberalism, and All I Got Was This Made-in-China T-Shirt

1. https://www.nar.realtor/sites/default/files/documents/2020 -international-transactions-in-us-residential-real-estate-08-06-2020.pdf
2. https://www.cnbc.com/2015/06/22/wealthy-foreigners-bought-100 -billion-in-us-real-estate.html
3. https://www.statista.com/statistics/611020/total-number-of-properties -purchased-by-chinese-buyers-in-the-us/
4. https://www.technocracy.news/foreigners-own-30-million-acres-of-prime -u-s-farmland/
5. Ibid.
6. https://www.law.nyu.edu/sites/default/files/Who's Left to Tax%3F US Taxation of Corporations and Their Shareholders- Rosenthal and Burke.pdf
7. https://www.investopedia.com/articles/markets-economy/090616/5 -countries-own-most-us-debt.asp
8. https://www.npr.org/2021/08/10/1026548591/too-much-import-too -little-export
9. https://www.forbes.com/sites/timworstall/2017/07/19/heres-that-trade -deficit-coming-back-foreigners-buy-more-us-houses/?sh=2f88f2c04375
10. https://www.macrotrends.net/countries/USA/united-states/trade -balance-deficit
11. https://www.macrotrends.net/countries/USA/united-states/trade -balance-deficit; https://www.usinflationcalculator.com/
12. https://www.macrotrends.net/countries/USA/united-states/trade -balance-deficit
13. https://www.macrotrends.net/countries/USA/united-states/trade -balance-deficit; https://www.usinflationcalculator.com/.
14. https://www.npr.org/sections/thetwo-way/2015/12/09/459087477/the -tipping-point-most-americans-no-longer-are-middle-class
15. https://www.industryweek.com/the-economy/article/22028495 /manufacturing-is-now-smallest-share-of-us-economy-in-72-years
16. Friedman, *The Lexus and the Olive Tree*.

Chapter 27. Neoliberal Trade Policy Rejected by South Korea

1. Peter Baker and Rachel Donadio, "Obama Wins More Food Aid but Presses African Nations on Corruption," *New York Times*, July 11, 2009, https:// www.nytimes.com/2009/07/11/world/europe/11prexy.html.
2. https://www.nytimes.com/2009/07/11/opinion/11sat1.html
3. Ha-Joon Chang, *Bad Samaritans: The Myth of Free Trade and the Secret History of Capitalism* (New York: Bloomsbury Press, 2008).

Chapter 28. Reverse Privatization of Core Government Functions

1. https://www.payscale.com/career-advice/average_salary__1-2/
2. https://www.washingtonpost.com/archive/politics/1997/05/10/private
-contractors-pick-up-kp-duty-for-us-troops-in-bosnia/6ee9893a-420c
-461a-88f4-e0fe1ea79868/
3. https://www.militarytimes.com/news/your-military/2021/07/30/dod
-really-has-no-idea-who-its-hired-to-do-private-security-report-finds/
4. https://www.pogo.org/analysis/2020/07/the-bunker-the-contractors-pie
-keeps-growing/
5. https://watson.brown.edu/costsofwar/files/cow/imce/papers/2020
/Peltier%202020%20-%20Growth%20of%20Camo%20Economy%20-%20
June%2030%202020%20-%20FINAL.pdf
6. Ibid.
7. https://s3.amazonaws.com/thf_media/1986/pdf/bg494.pdf
8. https://www.theguardian.com/world/2013/jun/10/edward-snowden
-booz-allen-hamilton-contractors

Chapter 30. Progressive Populism to Replace Progressive Neoliberalism

1. https://www.npr.org/2016/03/01/468185698/understanding-the
-clintons-popularity-with-black-voters
2. https://www.washingtonpost.com/news/the-fix/wp/2016/05/11/where
-democratic-voters-dont-like-either-hillary-clinton-or-bernie-sanders/
3. https://www.huffpost.com/entry/les-moonves-donald-trump_n
_56d52ce8e4b03260bf780275
4. https://www.thestreet.com/politics/donald-trump-rode-5-billion-in-free
-media-to-the-white-house-13896916

Chapter 31. Standing on the Edge

1. Antonio Gramsci, *Selections from the Prison Notebooks*, eds. Quintin Hoare and Geoffrey Nowell (New York: International Publishers Co., 1989 reprint ed., orig. pub. 1971), 276.
2. William Strauss and Neil Howe, *The Fourth Turning: An American Prophecy* (New York: Broadway Books, 1997).
3. Stephen Skowronek, *The Politics Presidents Make: Leadership from John Adams to Bill Clinton* (Cambridge, MA: Harvard University Press, 1997).
4. https://www.nytimes.com/2021/12/09/opinion/joe-biden-political-time
.html
5. Gramsci, *Selections from the Prison Notebooks*, 276.
6. https://www.nytimes.com/2021/12/09/opinion/joe-biden-political-time.html
7. Nancy Fraser, *The Old Is Dying and the New Cannot Be Born: From Progressive Neoliberalism to Trump and Beyond* (New York: Verso Books, 2019).

ACKNOWLEDGMENTS

At Berrett-Koehler Publishers, special thanks go to Steve Piersanti—who is the founder—and worked with me to kick off this series. It's been a labor of love for both of us, and I'm so grateful to Steve for his insights, rigor, and passion for this project. Of the many other people at BK who have helped with this book (and some projects associated with it), special thanks to Jeevan Sivasubramaniam (who has helped keep me sane for years) and Neal Maillet, a constant source of encouragement and wisdom. BK is an extraordinary publishing company, and it's been an honor to have them publish my books for almost two decades. And thanks to Tai Moses, who edited my *Thom Hartmann Reader* and returned to do a first pass with this book, for all her insights and help.

BK also provided a brilliant final editor for the book, Elissa Rabellino, who did a great job smoothing and tightening the text, production manager Linda Jupiter, who turned it into its final typeset form, and Mary Kanable, proofreader extraordinaire.

Bill Gladstone, my agent for over two decades, helped make this book—and the *Hidden History* series—possible. Bill is truly one of the best in the business.

INDEX

A

Allende Gossens, Salvador, 43–49
American Plan, viii, 9, 117–22
    Chinese version, 133–35, 136–40
    South Korean version, 141–44
    tenets of, 125–26
American Revolution, 8–9, 119–20, 156
Ames, Mark, 34
antitrust and antimonopoly laws, 93
Arab-Israeli War (1973), 53
The Arrow of Time (Conners), 63
Athens, 15
"austerity," 10, 36

B

*Bad Samaritans: The Myth of Free
    Trade and the Secret History of
    Capitalism* (Chang), 142
banking industry, 69, 74–78, 79, 90
Barofsky, Neil, 69
Bennett, Bill, 57
"best minds," as greediest minds, 99
Biden, Joe, 83, 152–53
Bipartisan Infrastructure bill, 103
Black vote, 149–50
Blair, Tony, 11
Bogle, Jack, 74–75
Bolsheviks, 8, 20
Bolton, John, 70
bookkeeping, 14
Bork, Robert, 61
Bremer, L. Paul, III, 71–72
Bretton Woods framework, 51
Brown, Sherrod, 68, 139
Brown v. Board of Education, 57
Bush, George H. W., 55, 64
Bush, George W., vii, 68–73, 74, 150
Bush, Jeb, 70
"Bush Crash" of 2008, 69–70, 75–77,
    90, 138
Business Plot, 9

C

Calhoun, John C., 115
Cambodia, 8
Capital in the Twenty-First Century.
    (Piketty), 113
capitalism
    democracy as threat to, 3–4, 17–18,
      33
    free-market, 14–15
Carter, Jimmy, 54, 55
The Case Against Socialism (Paul), 27
Castro, Sergio de, 47
Central Intelligence Agency (CIA),
    43–45
CEO salaries, 11, 58, 113–14, 147
Chang, Ha-Joon, 142
Cheney, Dick, 70
Chicago School, 64, 146
Chile, vii, 11, 39, 41, 42–50
    Chicago Boys, vii, 39, 46–47, 65
    and Friedman, 47–50
    Gran Minería companies, 42–43
    privatization, 47–48
    US-led coup, 45–46
China, viii, 132, 136–40
    escape from neoliberalism, 133–
      35, 136
    free trade with, 86–87
    housing purchases, 136–37
    plans, 134
A Christmas Carol (Dickens), 111–12
citizenship, as secondary, 39
Civil War, 9, 156
Clinton, Bill, 10–11, 49, 60–67, 86–87,
    96, 139, 149–50
Clinton, Hillary, 139, 151
collateralized debt obligations
    (CDOs), 69, 76–77
commons, privatization of, 98–106
communism, 1–2, 15–16, 24, 34–35
Communist Party, Italy, 155

Communist Party of China, 133–34
Conners, Leila, 63
conservative populism, 150–52
conservatives, 115–16
consumers, citizens as, 39
Cornwall, Rupert, 46
corporations
    fascist Italy, 1–2
    and social responsibility, 34–35
Costa Rica, 89
cost-benefit estimates, 56–57, 96
"Costs of War" research project, 146
Council on Foreign Relations, 128
COVID pandemic, 92, 94, 137, 139
cycles of history, 155–56

D

Das Kapital (Marx), 15–16
democracy, 3–4, 15, 17–18, 33, 106–7
Democratic Party, 53, 61, 80, 149–51
democratic socialism, 17, 22–30, 63
Deng Xiaoping, viii, 133–34, 140
deregulation, viii–ix, 33, 36, 55, 69,
    75, 82
direct foreign investment, 136–37
Dodd, Christopher, 80
Dodd-Frank legislation, 80
dollar, 51–53, 136
Donovan, Ray, 58

E

East India Company, 119–20
Economic Growth, Regulatory Relief,
    and Consumer Protection Act,
    82
education, 3, 18, 57, 89–90
Electoral College, 139, 152
Emergency Economic Stabilization
    Act, 79
employment, 58, 62, 80, 91, 100

England, 117–20
environment, 57, 96–97
Executive Order 12291 (cost-benefit
    estimate), 56

F

factories, United States, 52, 58
Fairness Doctrine and Equal Time
    Rule, 95
fascism, 1–5, 9
    neoliberal views of, 19–20, 24–25,
        26, 39, 107
    white-power neofascism, 155, 156,
        158
Federal Reserve, 77–78, 90, 92, 110
feudalism, 8, 13–14, 15
finance, 90
financial services industry, 69, 74–76
Financial Services Modernization Act
    (FSMA), 67
Fisher, Antony, 55
Ford, Gerald, 53–54
Foundation for Economic Education
    (FEE), 33–34
Fourth Amendment, 101
The Fourth Turning (Strauss and
    Howe), 155–56
France, 8
Franco, Francisco, 1
Frank, Barney, 80
Franklin, Benjamin, 98, 104
Fraser, Nancy, 158
Freedom of Information Act, 101
"free market," 3, 11, 14–15, 32, 131
    and autocracies, 86–87
    as superior to government, 37–38
free trade agreements, 62, 121–22
    North American Free Trade
        Agreement (NAFTA), 55, 58,
        60, 121

Friedman, Milton, viii, 10, 17, 30–35, 133, 146
  and Bush, 70, 71
  and Chile, 47–50
  and Howe, 54–55
  Works
    Capitalism and Freedom, 31–35
    " Occupational Licensure" chapter, 32–33
    Roofs or Ceilings? The Current Housing Problem, 34
Friedman, Thomas, viii–ix, 62, 86, 127
  The Lexus and the Olive Tree: Understanding Globalization, 140, 143–44
  "Tangled Trade Talks," 142
From, Al, 61
fundamentalists, 57

G

Gandhi, Mahatma, 120
Geithner, Timothy, 80
General Agreement on Tariffs and Trade (GATT), 121
General Motors, 112, 113
Germany, 23–25, 141
gig economy, 80
Giroux, Henry, 84
Glass-Steagall Act, 67, 80, 90
gold standard, 51–52
Goldwater, Barry, 30
Gorbachev, Mikhail, 63–64, 67
Gorsuch, Anne, 57
government, privatization of, 37–38, 145–47
Gramsci, Antonio, 155, 157–58
Great Britain, 22–23
Great Depression, Republican, 9, 23, 50, 132, 149, 156
Great Recession of 2008, 138.
  See also "Bush Crash" of 2008

Greek nation-states, 15
Gulf Wars, 71

H

Halliburton Company, 70
Hamilton, Alexander, viii, 9, 117–22, 123–24, 140
  on goods made in America, 129–32.
    See also American Plan
Hayek, F. A., 7, 10, 19, 119
  vs. birth of democratic socialism, 22–30
  Works
    Law, Legislation and Liberty, 16–17
    The Road to Serfdom, 23, 25, 28–30
health care, 18, 24, 68, 79, 88–89, 100, 150
hedge funds, 75, 92, 96, 104
Henry VII, 117–18, 140
Herskowitz, Mickey, 70–71
Hinsdale, Daniel, 120
Hitler, Adolf, 1, 7, 19–20, 22, 27, 160n4
homelessness, 92–93
housing
  foreign purchases of, 136–37
  mortgages, 69, 70, 75–77
How China Escaped Shock Therapy (Weber), 134
Howe, Geoffrey, 54–55
Howe, Neil, 155–56
Hume, David, 115
Hungary, 108–9, 153

I

imports and exports, 52, 117–18, 125–26
index funds, 74–75
India, 120
"individual responsibility," 89
inequality, 11, 14, 39, 112, 114
  Chile, 49–50

inflation, 36, 39, 51–56, 93–94
Institute of Economic Affairs (IEA),
    54–55
International Telephone & Telegraph
    (ITT), 44, 45
In the Public Interest study, 100
"invisible hand," 15, 69, 77, 119, 153
Iraq, 70–73
Islam, Faisal, 87
Italy, 1–2, 155

J

Jacksonian regime (1828 to 1860), 156
Japan, 141, 143–44
Jefferson, Thomas, 13, 32, 36, 94, 104,
    122, 124
Jeffersonian regime (1800 to 1828), 156

K

Kaliningrad, Russia, 65–66
Kandell, Jonathan, 46
Kennedy, John F., 30–31
Kennedy, Robert, 150
Kenya, 141, 142
Keynesian model, 10, 116, 123, 149
Kissinger, Henry, 43, 45
Klein, Lawrence, 63
Klein, Naomi, 35, 49, 64
Knox, Henry, 119
Kornbluh, Peter, 50
Kristol, Bill, 70
Krynen, Will, 8

L

Labor Department, 57–58
Law, Legislation and Liberty (Hayek),
    16–17
Lay, Ken, 69
Lee, Mike, 68
Lehman Brothers, 78
Lenin, Vladimir, 8

Lexus (Toyota), 143–44
liar loans, 75–76
liberalism, as term, 17
Libertarian Party, 33
libraries, public, 98–99
Library Systems and Services
    (LS&S), 98–99, 105
licensure, 32–33, 38–39
Lincoln, Abraham, 18, 127
Lindbergh, Charles, 10
Lippmann, Walter, 17
living-wage jobs, 91
Li Yining, 134
looting, neoliberal, 72

M

Manchin, Joe, 83, 103
manufacturing, 125–26, 129–32
    factories lost, 127–28
    South Korea, 142–43
Mao Zedong, 133
Mareschal, Patrice M., 102
"market interference," 91
Marx, Karl, 2, 15–16, 25
Marxism, Hitler's view of, 27–28
means of production, state ownership
    of, 25
media and news, 4, 94–96, 101, 151
medical profession, 32–33, 38–39
Medicare, vii, 37, 68–69, 79, 83, 150
mergers and acquisitions, 93
middle class, 9, 24, 56, 85, 91, 110, 138
    rebuilding, 111–16
    Russia, 64–65
    working poor, 113–14.
        See also working class
Milanovic, Branko, 50
"military contractors," 145–46
Milken, Michael, 93
Mises, Ludwig von, 10, 17, 19–23

Mnuchin, Steven, 69, 78
monopolies, 39, 130, 148
Montalva, Eduardo Frei, 42
Mont Pelerin Society, 1–5, 17–18, 22,
    54–55, 71
Moonves, Les, 151
Moore, Stephen, 18, 146–47, 161n8
"moral order," 4–5
Mussolini, Benito, 1–2, 155

N
National Party (Chile), 43
National Socialism (Nazism), 3, 7, 10,
    23–30
nation-states, 13, 15
Nazi Cell (Chilean army), 45
Nelson, Herbert, 33–34
neoliberalism
    American awareness of, 12, 78, 139,
        140, 150
    birth of, 13–18
    breaking with 40 years of, 108–9
    challenges to, 149–54
    China's escape from, 133–35
    drawing to a close, 153
    military, effect on, 145–47
    racism as central to, 19–22
    tenets of, 36–40
    as term, vii, 5
New Deal order (1932 to 1980), 23,
    156, 157
New Democrat Caucus, 11
The New Russia: Transition Gone Awry
    (Klein and Pomer), 63–64
Nichols, Caleb, 98, 104–5
Nixon, Richard, 43–45, 51–54, 149
Nixon administration, 47
North American Free Trade
    Agreement (NAFTA), 55, 58, 60,
    121, 140

O
Obama, Barack, 79–80, 141, 150
*The Old Is Dying and the New Cannot
    Be Born* (Fraser), 158
oligarchs, 9, 12, 18, 39, 65, 72–73, 108–9
Orbán, Viktor, 108–9
oversight, 101–2

P
Park Chung-hee, 142
Paul, Rand, 27, 38–39
Paul, Ron, 68
Peltier, Heidi, 146
Perot, Ross, 60–61, 68, 140
philanthropy, 67
Piketty, Thomas, 85, 113
Pinochet, Augusto, vii, 42–50
The Pinochet File (Kornbluh), 50
The Politics Presidents Make
    (Skowronek), 156
Pol Pot, 8
Pomer, Marshall, 63
Popper, Karl, 7
populism
    conservative, 150–52
    progressive, 150–54
Portman, Rob, 103
poverty, 11, 43, 50, 64, 100
Powel, Elizabeth Willing, 98
prison industry, 102–3
"privacy, right of," 101–2
privatization, 10, 25, 37
    Chile, 47–48
    of commons, 98–106
    of government, 37–38, 145–47
progressive populism, 150–51, 156–57
Project for a New American Century
    statement, 70
propaganda, 29–30
property rights, 37

protectionist policies, 120, 123, 142–44
Prussianism, 26–27
public information laws, 101
"public-private partnerships," 103
public-sector government jobs, 100
Putin, Vladimir, 63, 67, 108–9

R
racism, 19–22, 149, 150, 157
Rand, Ayn, 38
Reagan, Ronald, ix, 10, 11, 18, 30, 55–56, 85, 93, 99, 138–39
Reagan order (1980 to current), 156–57
Reagan Revolution (1981)/ Reaganomics, 10, 36, 41, 112, 127
real estate industry, 33–34, 70
recession of 2006, 76
regimes, 155–59
Reich, Robert, 94
Report on the Subject of Manufactures (Hamilton), 117, 121, 125, 129–32
Republican Party, 32, 80, 81–82, 106, 115–16, 151
Republican regime (1860 to 1932), 156
The Road to Serfdom (Hayek), 23, 25, 28–30
Robin, Corey, 156, 158
Roosevelt, Franklin D., 9–10, 23, 140, 153–54
"rugged individualism," 88, 104
Rumsfeld, Donald, 70–72
Rush, Benjamin, 13, 39
Russia, viii, 1, 8, 11, 20, 41, 64–65, 108–9, 135

S
Sanders, Bernie, 68, 83, 108, 138–39, 150–51, 153
service economy, 62, 123, 139
"seventh generation" concept, 97

The Shock Doctrine (Klein), 35, 49, 64
"shock neoliberalism," 37, 133–35
Sinema, Kyrsten, 83
Skowronek, Stephen, 156
Smith, Adam, 15, 118–19, 123
Smith, Morgan, 101
Smithfield Foods, 137
Snowden, Edward, 104, 147
social democracy, 17, 28
socialism
    Friedman's view of, 34, 48
    Hitler's view of, 27–28
    "scientific," 7
social movements, 115–16
social responsibility, as "communism," 34–35
South Korea, 141–44
Soviet Union, viii, 1–3, 7, 25, 63–64, 92–93
Spencer, Herbert, 86
Stewart, Emily, 151
Stigler, George, 146
Strauss, William, 155–56
Summers, Lawrence, 80, 94
Supreme Court, 61

T
Taft, William H., 57–58
"Tangled Trade Talks" (New York Times), 142
tariffs, viii, 51, 72, 82, 114, 117–21
    America built by, 127–28
    South Korea, 142–43
taxes, 14, 32, 72, 84–85, 109, 110, 114
    Biden's attempt to reverse cuts, 152–53
    cuts for the rich, 10, 56, 85, 152–53, 157
    neoliberal view of, 37–40
Tea Act of 1773, 120
telecommunications laws, 44, 95–96

Thatcher, Margaret, viii–ix, 10, 25, 31–32, 54–55, 88

Third Way, 10–11

Thomson, Charles, 119

"The Tipping Point: Most Americans No Longer Are Middle Class" (NPR), 110

"Top 1% of U.S. Earners Now Hold More Wealth Than All of the Middle Class" (Bloomberg), 110

totalitarianism, 7, 16, 18, 26, 29

Toyota, 143–44

trade, 85–87, 109, 138

"trade secrets," 101

trade unions, 33, 39, 54–55, 58, 61, 91, 105

transparency laws, 147

Treasuries, owned by China, 137

Troubled Asset Relief Program (TARP), 69, 79

Trump, Donald, 11, 18, 67, 78, 81–82, 108, 137–39, 153, 155–56

Trump University, 75–76

"Tudor Plan" (Henry VII), 117–18

U

unemployment, 39, 50, 76, 104

United Kingdom, 10, 11, 54–55

United States
    American Revolution, 8–9, 119–20, 156
    bifurcation of, 158
    and Chile, 42
    factories, 52, 58
    gross domestic product (GDP), 84
    inflation, 51–54, 55–56
    infrastructure, 152
    Reagan Revolution (1981), 36, 41

V

"value for money" stipulation, 103

Volcker Alliance, 99

voters, 115, 149–50

W

Wall Street (movie), 56

Walmart, 112, 100, 128, 132

Walton, Sam, 128

Warren, Elizabeth, 153

Washington, George, viii, 9, 117, 119–20, 125

Watergate scandal, 53

Watt, James, 57

The Wealth of Nations (Smith), 15, 118–19

Weber, Isabella M., 134

welfare programs, gutting of, 62–63

welfare state, 23–25, 37, 49

"When Private Firms Run Schools, Financial Secrecy Is Allowed" (Smith), 101

Whip Inflation Now (WIN), 54

white neoliberal imperialism, 19–22, 155, 156, 158

Wolfowitz, Paul, 70

working class, 41, 91, 112, 113–14, 126, 135, 157

World Economic Forum, 67

World Trade Organization (WTO), 87, 122

World War II, 113, 145, 156

Y

"Year One"/"Year Zero," 8

Yeltsin, Boris, 67

Z

Zhao Ziyang, viii, 134, 140

Zhirinovsky, Vladimir, 66–67

ABOUT THE AUTHOR

© Ian Sbalcio

Thom Hartmann is a four-time Project Censored Award–winning, *New York Times* best-selling author and America's number one progressive talk show host. He and his wife, Louise, live with three cats and two dogs on the Columbia River in Portland, Oregon.

BOOKS BY THOM HARTMANN

The Hidden History of Big Brother in America: How the Death of Privacy and the Rise of Surveillance Threaten Us and Our Democracy

The Hidden History of American Healthcare: Why Sickness Bankrupts You and Makes Others Insanely Rich

The Hidden History of American Oligarchy: Reclaiming Our Democracy from the Ruling Class

The Hidden History of Monopolies: How Big Business Destroyed the American Dream

The Hidden History of the War on Voting: Who Stole Your Vote and How to Get It Back

The Hidden History of Guns and the Second Amendment

The Hidden History of the Supreme Court and the Betrayal of America

Adult ADHD: How to Succeed as a Hunter in a Farmer's World

The Last Hours of Ancient Sunlight: The Fate of the World and What We Can Do Before It's Too Late

Unequal Protection: How Corporations Became "People"—and How You Can Fight Back

The Crash of 2016: The Plot to Destroy America—and What We Can Do to Stop It

Screwed: The Undeclared War Against the Middle Class—and What We Can Do About It

Rebooting the American Dream: 11 Ways to Rebuild Our Country

The Thom Hartmann Reader

Walking Your Blues Away: How to Heal the Mind and Create Emotional Well-Being

The Prophet's Way: A Guide to Living in the Now

Legacy of Secrecy: The Long Shadow of the JFK Assassination (with Lamar Waldron)

Cracking the Code: How to Win Hearts, Change Minds, and Restore America's Original Vision

We the People: A Call to Take Back America

What Would Jefferson Do?: A Return to Democracy

Threshold: The Progressive Plan to Pull America Back from the Brink

The Last Hours of Humanity: Warming the World to Extinction

The American Revolution of 1800: How Jefferson Rescued Democracy from Tyranny and Faction (with Dan Sisson)

ADD Success Stories: A Guide to Fulfillment for Families with Attention Deficit Disorder

Ultimate Sacrifice: John and Robert Kennedy, the Plan for a Coup in Cuba, and the Murder of JFK (with Lamar Waldron)

Attention Deficit Disorder: A Different Perception

Think Fast: The ADD Experience

Healing ADD: Simple Exercises That Will Change Your Daily Life

Thom Hartmann's Complete Guide to ADHD: Help for Your Family at Home, School, and Work

From the Ashes: A Spiritual Response to the Attack on America (anthology)

Beyond ADD: Hunting for Reasons in the Past and Present

Berrett–Koehler
Publishers

Dear reader,

Thank you for picking up this book and welcome to the worldwide BK community! You're joining a special group of people who have come together to create positive change in their lives, organizations, and communities.

What's BK all about?

Our mission is to connect people and ideas to create a world that works for all.

Why? Our communities, organizations, and lives get bogged down by old paradigms of self-interest, exclusion, hierarchy, and privilege. But we believe that can change. That's why we seek the leading experts on these challenges—and share their actionable ideas with you.

A welcome gift

To help you get started, we'd like to offer you a free copy of one of our bestselling ebooks:

www.bkconnection.com/welcome

When you claim your **free ebook,** you'll also be subscribed to our blog.

Our freshest insights

Access the best new tools and ideas for leaders at all levels on our blog at ideas.bkconnection.com.

Sincerely,

Your friends at Berrett-Koehler

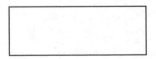

Certified

Corporation